David Smith
The Formative Years

Sculptures and Drawings from the 1930s and 1940s

Karen Wilkin

The Edmonton Art Gallery

The Edmonton Art Gallery is a registered, non-profit society
supported by memberships and donations, and by grants from the
City of Edmonton, Alberta Culture, the Canada Council, and the
Museum Assistance Programmes of The National Museums of
Canada.

© The Edmonton Art Gallery, 1981
  ISBN 0-88950-016-9

The Edmonton Art Gallery
2 Sir Winston Churchill Square
Edmonton, Alberta T5J 2C1

Contents

Itinerary

The Edmonton Art Gallery - Edmonton, Alberta
January 16 - March 1, 1981

Seattle Art Museum - Seattle, Washington
March 19 - May 10, 1981

The Winnipeg Art Gallery - Winnipeg, Manitoba
August 14 - September 26, 1981

Art Gallery of Hamilton - Hamilton, Ontario
October 15 - November 15, 1981

Art Gallery of Windsor - Windsor, Ontario
December 6 - January 17, 1982

Acknowledgements

I would like to thank all lenders to this exhibition for their generosity, and the staff of The Edmonton Art Gallery for their invaluable assistance and support. Special thanks are due to Terry Fenton, Maggie Callahan, Russell Bingham and Sandra Shaul, whose tireless efforts have made it possible for this exhibition and this catalogue to exist.

I am grateful to the Trustees of the David Smith Estate for their early support of the project and for making material available to me, to Marian Moffatt of the Knoedler Gallery and to Ada Bortoluzzi of the Fogg Museum for their patience and help, and to the Archives of American Art for their rich resources. Thanks, too, to Hank Talkington for his photographs of David Smith at Bolton Landing.

My particular thanks to Shirley Matzke, Curator of the David Smith Estate, and Rebecca and Candida Smith, whose knowledge and enthusiasm have been so generously given to the preparation of this exhibition. I deeply appreciate all of their hard work and kindness. I am forever indebted to Dorothy Dehner who, in a very special way, has immeasurably enriched both this exhibition and my experience. Finally, I would like to thank Donald Clinton for his skill as an editor, among other things.

David Smith and a neighbour at Bolton Landing, New York, 1946

4

Introduction

Every year, David Smith's reputation grows a little. Every new showing of his work makes him loom larger — as a giant of American art, of sculpture, of the 20th century. But even if Smith's achievement is uncontested, and even if a great deal has been written about him, there are still aspects of his work which are not well known. His last burnished steel pieces, the Cubi, are conspicuous enough, and a recent show of the early 60s Voltris[1] helped to acquaint people with this superb series, but most of Smith's early, formative sculptures have received less attention. Yet these, some of his most provocative and mysterious works, explore images and formal concerns which preoccupied him throughout his career.

Despite this apparent singlemindedness, though, that career is full of contradictions. Perhaps the most basic is that although Smith has been given his place in the history of contemporary art as a sculptor in metal, he insisted that he "belonged with painters." He liked to reinforce this apparent paradox by pointing out that much of the best modern sculpture has been made by painters: Picasso, Matisse, Degas.[2] Smith publically declared: "And I never conceived of myself as anything other than a painter, because my work came right through the surface and color and objects applied to the surface."[3]

Smith's development is, in fact, a kind of home grown recapitulation of the evolution of modernist constructed sculpture from Cubist painting and collage. The story is familiar now. As a young painter, a student in Jan Matulka's influential class at the Art Students League, Smith began to affix things to his canvases, turning them into reliefs and eventually into three-dimensional constructions. He described the process, when he took part in a symposium on *The New Sculpture:*

> While my technical liberation came from Picasso's friend and countryman, Gonzalez, my aesthetics were more influenced by Kandinsky, Mondrian, and Cubism. My student period was only involved with paintings. The painting developed into raised levels from the canvas. Gradually, the canvas became the base and the painting was a sculpture.[4]

There is an equally familiar litany which goes along with this story: because Smith was trained not as a sculptor, but as a painter, he was able to avoid sculptural clichés, and claim new territory for sculpture. There's some truth in this, of course, but it's also important to keep in mind that even if Smith *had* been studying sculpture formally, there were almost no new, inventive examples to be seen in New York at the time he started to work in three dimensions. Because he had so little first hand experience of advanced sculpture, he was more or less forced to make it up as he went along. Which is not to say Smith had no ancestors, or that he didn't find clues in a great variety of sources. His inventions were firmly based in what he knew and had seen of many kinds of art (and some non-art). He drew on the tradition of Western painting, African carving, Egyptian tomb furnishings, a little sculpture, and almost anything else he came in contact with.

A good deal has been written about Smith's connections with his sources. It goes without saying that he owed an enormous debt to the legacy of Picasso, and to Gonzalez, Giacometti, Gargallo and Miro, among others. It's fascinating, of course, to explore Smith's relationship to his predecessors, but it's perhaps even more fascinating to focus on what is his own.

The works Smith made between 1933 — when he made his first welded metal pieces — and 1950 — when his sculpture shifted dramatically in scale — are stamped with both the traces of his chosen ancestors and the mark of his unique invention. They reveal Smith to be one of the most idiosyncratic and rigorous of sculptors, one of the most willful, yet one of the most receptive to suggestions from his materials and from unexpected sources.

Early Years

David Roland Smith was raised in small mid-western American towns. Born in Decatur, Indiana, in 1906, he was 15 when his family moved to Paulding, Ohio. Like Jackson Pollock and Clyfford Still, Smith was one of those curious beings who grow up more or less isolated from important painting or sculpture, but know they want to make art. Pollock, at least, had the advantage of a sympathetic art teacher at his high school in Los Angeles, and the example of older brothers studying at the Art Students League and Columbia University. Smith's early experience was more limited:

> I don't think I had seen a museum out in Indiana or Ohio other than some very, very dark picture with sheep in it in the public library. I didn't know anything about art until I came to New York. [But] I wanted to be a painter when I came.[5]

As Paul Cummings has pointed out, in his catalogue, *David Smith: The Drawings,*[6] Smith's early facility as a cartoonist won him praise at Paulding High School. He was ambitious enough about his drawing to subscribe to a correspondence course — probably for lack of anything better close at hand. When he spent a year at Ohio University, in 1924, he gave most of his attention to studying art. The following year Smith transferred to Notre Dame, but left after two weeks when he discovered no art courses were available. During the summer of 1925, between his brief bouts of higher education, Smith worked at the Studebaker Plant in South Bend, Indiana. He described the job as "riveter on frame assembly, worked on lathe — soldering jig — spot welder. Did it strictly for money — more than I ever earned in my life."[7]

In 1952, Smith spoke about the role this factory stint had played in his life as a sculptor:

> Before knowing what art was or before going to art school, as a factory worker I was acquainted with steel and the machines used in forging it. During my second year in art school I learned about Cubism, Picasso and Gonzalez through *Cahiers d'art.* From them I learned that art was being made with steel — the material and machines that had previously meant only labor and earning power.[8]

Although Smith liked to trace his identification with "the working man" and his skill as a metal worker back to his early days at Studebaker, he, in fact, quickly shifted from a blue collar to a white collar position when he returned to the company after dropping out of Notre Dame. Smith joined Studebaker's finance department, not the assembly line. His next job, with a cooperative banking plan company, brought him to Washington, D.C. and one more semester of college, studying poetry at Georgetown University. In 1926, the company sent Smith to New York, where he found a room near Columbia University. He asked his landlady about art schools, and she referred him to another tenant, a young woman named Dorothy Dehner who was away visiting her family in California. Dehner recalls that as soon as she returned, Smith introduced himself brusquely and demanded advice. She recommended the Art Students League, where she was studying.[9] Dehner's suggestion suited Smith; he remained at the League for five years, studying with John Sloan, Jan Matulka and Kymon Nicolaides.

Dehner's influence on Smith is incalculable. She was thoroughly familiar with some of the most advanced music, dance, art and literature of the time, and had travelled a great deal, even on her own in Europe, in the '20s. (She has had a distinguished career as a painter and sculptor, in her own right.) Her upbringing had been unconventional: orphaned as a child, she was raised by her rather Chekhovian aunts in Pasadena. It seems likely that her combination of intelligence, sophistication and remarkable good looks stood for everything Smith's own experience had failed to provide. They married in December of 1927, and stayed together for nearly twenty five years, until their divorce in 1952. Smith was aware of his debt to Dorothy Dehner. Writing to her in June 1944, he stated: "I owe my direction to you."[10]

Through friends at the League, the Smiths met the painter John Graham, a considerable presence in New York's "underground" art world of the late '20s and the '30s. An emigré member of the minor Russian nobility,[11] Graham had lived in Paris as an artist and as a kind of private dealer, and had come to know an astonishing cross section of the European avant garde. He was familiar with the most radical art being made at the time — Picasso's latest works, Gonzalez, the Surrealists — and his annual trips to France provided his artist friends in New York with first hand information, reinforcing the modernist teachings of Jan Matulka at the League. He was also a connnoisseur and collector of primitive art, and advised collectors of African sculpture.[12]

Around 1930, it was Graham who gave Smith copies of French art magazines, including issues of *Cahiers d'art* with illustrated articles on the welded metal sculpture of Picasso and Gonzalez. It was also Graham who, in 1933, provided Smith with an opportunity to study a fine group of African carvings, by having him hired to make the bases for the Frank Crowninshield collection (which Graham had selected). Smith lived with the sculptures, storing them in his apartment while he worked on them.

Graham's concerns were wide ranging. His 1937 book, *System and Dialectics of Art,* which seems an accurate reflection of his conversation, distills then current ideas about creativity, Marx, psychoanalysis, the alienation of the artist, taste, primivitism and abstraction — and even such abstruse problems as the relation of art and crime, genius and suicide. For Graham, art was "a creative process of abstracting," "a systemic confession of personality."[13] It originated in "the human longing for enigma,"[14] and its purpose was to "reestablish lost contact with the unconscious and the primordial racial past."[15] Graham expressed similar ideas in an article entitled "Primitive Art and Picasso," in the April 1937 issue of *Magazine of Art.*

He stressed that "our unconscious mind contains a record of all our past experiences — individual and racial"; this concept of a collective unconscious, being, of course, fundamental to the work of Carl Jung, who Graham cited along with Freud, as a source, in *System and Dialectics of Art.* It is a central theme in the book, inextricably bound up, for Graham, with creativity itself. Obviously, Graham was not the only source of these ideas, no matter how powerful or persuasive he was as a talker. The theories of Freud and Jung, the role of myth and symbol, the relation between creativity and neurosis, were all current topics among the intellectually curious of New York in the '30s.[16] In the same way, the Leftist beliefs which the Smiths espoused were also current coin among the sensitive and thoughtful, a reaction to the social and economic upheavals of the period.

David Smith and Dorothy Dehner, December 1927

There were opportunities to see a small amount of provocative new art in New York, at the time, as well as talk about it, although the city was far from being a center where innovative art was easily seen. When Smith first arrived, in the late 20s, his teachers at the League — Sloan and especially the European-trained Matulka, to whom Smith gave most credit as an influence — transmitted ideas about Cubism, Constructivism and abstraction. Some modernist work was exhibited at galleries such as Stieglitz's Intimate Gallery, Dudensing, Wildenstein, and a few rather shakey institutions dedicated to "the new movements in the arts," such as The Art Center, The Little Review Gallery and the New Art Circle.[17] The Museum of Modern Art wasn't founded until 1929.

By the '30s though, a greater variety of influences was at work. The best information still came from European magazines like the *Transitions* and *Cahiers d'art* that Graham had shown Smith, but even the conservative *American Magazine of Art* reproduced work by Klee, Kandinsky, Gonzalez and Dali. Exhibitions at the new Museum of Modern Art and the few commercial galleries committed to the modern movement provided New Yorkers with more direct experience of radical ideas. Dorothy Dehner recalls the eagerness with which young artists visited these shows: "We looked at everyone we could see. We were hungry."[18]

By the '30s, too, the Smiths were part of a small group of forward looking younger artists. Some, like Edgar Levy and his wife, the illustrator Lucille Corcos, the Adolph Gottliebs and the Milton Averys, were the Smiths' close friends and neighbors in Brooklyn Heights. Levy, whom Dehner describes as "a real intellectual,"[19] was evidently a thoughful and well-read

Portraits of the Artists
Top row:
Lucille Corcos by Dorothy Dehner; David Smith by Lucille Corcos; Adolph Gottlieb by Edgar Levy
Bottom row:
Edgar Levy by Esther Gottlieb; Dorothy Dehner by Adolph Gottlieb; Esther Gottlieb by David Smith
(etching made in Edgar Levy's studio, Brooklyn Heights, New York, 1933)

man who rarely showed his (quite radical) paintings. Like Graham, he seems to have acted as a source of information and current ideas. Through Graham, too, the Smiths met other adventurous artists: Stuart Davis, Jean Xceron, Arshile Gorky and Willem de Kooning. Smith credited Xceron with having convinced him to focus his energies on sculpture:

Remember May, 1935, when we walked down 57th Street after your show . . . how you influenced me to concentrate on sculpture. I'm of course forever glad that you did, it's more my energy, though I make two hundred color drawings a year and sometimes painting . . . but I paint and draw as a sculptor. I have no split identity as I did in 1935.[20]

Smith, Graham, Davis, de Kooning, and Levy even formed a short-lived group in 1935. Their only action, Smith recalled, "was to notify the Whitney Museum

that we were a group and would only exhibit in the 1935 abstract show if all were asked. Some of us were, some exhibited, some didn't and that ended our group."[21]

It's clear that although Smith was probably accurate in crediting Dorothy Dehner with providing most of the "faith and encouragement in the formative years,"[22] he was also part of a stimulating group of likeminded artists who shared a common enthusiasm for modernism. Modernism, at the time, of course meant innovative European art. There were no American models of the stature of the inventors of Cubism or Fauvism or Surrealism. The handful of American painters who had gone to Europe and participated in the cataclysmic rethinking of what art could be, before World War I — such as Max Weber, Alfred Maurer and Marsden Hartley — had returned, retreated or become invisible. Only a few older American modernists — John Marin, Georgia O'Keeffe and Joseph Stella, for example — exhibited regularly in New York, but their work didn't come close to embodying the modern spirit to Smith's generation, the way Picasso's did. "Official" American art was neither modernist nor did it look to Europe: there was the self-conscious regionalism of the Thomas Hart Benton variety, which Smith's friend Adolph Gottlieb once described as the "Corn Belt Academy,"[23] and the engagé social realism which was its urban equivalent. And, perhaps, more importantly for Smith, advanced sculpture was even more rare than advanced painting. He certainly knew the few Americans who were attempting to make challenging sculpture, such as Ibram Lassaw and Alexander Calder, but he seemed uninterested in their work.

Years later, Gottlieb described his feelings during his early days:

. . . a few painters were painting with a feeling of absolute desperation . . . the situation was so bad that I know I felt free to try anything, no matter how absurd it seemed; what was there to lose? Neither Cubism nor Surealism could absorb someone like myself: we felt like derelicts.[24]

Smith's recollection of the '30s is only slightly less bleak:

One did not feel disowned — only ignored and much alone, with a vague pressure from authority that art couldn't be made here.[25]

Yet in 1936, Smith, along with Milton Avery, Willem de Kooning and Edgar Levy, was mentioned by John Graham as one of the few "young outstanding American painters," in *System and Dialectics of Art,*[26] and in January, 1938, Smith's first one man show of sculpture and drawings, opened at the Willard Gallery.

1930s

The 1930s marked the beginning of Smith's career as a sculptor, his beginning to make sculpture in metal, and his first long trips away from New York. In 1931, he and Dorothy Dehner "escaped" to the Virgin Islands, where they remained for eight months, until June 1932. Dehner explains the visit by saying: "We wanted to be Gauguin," which Smith's informal autobiography confirms.[27] His first completely free-standing sculptures, fragile constructions of wire and coral, were made at this time. They seem to have more to do with recognizing humanoid qualities in lumps of coral than with construction, but they could be said to prefigure Smith's later use of found objects and his uncanny ability to animate even the most unprepossessing of these objects. One of the earliest coral sculptures may have been Smith's first painted sculpture (although he had, of course, used polychromy in his early paintings-cum-constructions). Dehner remembers a "carved white coral head of a negro" which Smith painted "a purplish brown," as the second free-standing sculpture that he made.[28]

In 1933 at his Bolton Landing property, a former fox farm near Glens Falls which the couple had bought in 1929, Smith made a series of welded steel heads using found objects. They include this exhibition's *Agricola Head* (Fig. 1) and *Saw Head* (Fig. 2), which simultaneously allude to the figure and to general sculptural ideas of collaging, caging and layering. There's an obvious debt to Gonzalez's heads which Smith saw illustrated in *Cahiers d'art*,[29] particularly in the way in which the logic of human structure is obeyed despite the essentially abstract forms of the sculptures. A small group of constructed sculptures

made of wood, wire, metal and coral also dates from this period. Their combination of materials recalls "classic" Cubist collage, while their structure shows the influence of Henri Laurens, whose wooden constructions were also reproduced in *Cahiers d'art*. Yet the oddly uninterrupted contours of the sculptures, the way linear elements link solid forms, are remarkably close to Smith's idiosyncratic drawings.

On his return to the Brooklyn Heights apartment Smith continued to work in metal, making small scale welded sculptures which developed more complex figurations than the single heads of the previous summer. Dehner remembers following Smith around with a sprinkling can to quench welding sparks which threatened to set fire to the drawings tacked to the walls of their small living room-cum-studio. Shortly afterwards, he moved into Terminal Iron Works, the commercial welding shop where he found space to work and professional metalworkers who improved his welding technique and sometimes even provided material to work with.[30]

In 1935, Smith and Dorothy Dehner spent almost a year in Europe. This was his first European trip, and he saw and absorbed an extraordinary amount. On their arrival in Paris, Graham immediately took the Smiths to see an exhibition at Galerie Simon. Dorothy Dehner wrote to Lucille Corcos:

> (We) saw the newest Picasso, hot off the easel. Entirely different from any he has done before. Not very abstract in general conception but part abstractly painted — leaves for hands and so on — very heavy paint — quite rough.[31]

When Graham subsequently offered to introduce them to Picasso, Smith refused. As Dehner recalls: "He

Julio Gonzalez
L'Arlequin, c. 1927-29
cast bronze of welded iron original
42 cm high
Collection of the Kunsthaus,
Zurich

Agricola Head, 1933
iron and steel, painted red
46.7 x 25.7 x 19.7 cm
Collection of The Estate of David
Smith
*Courtesy of M. Knoedler and Co.,
New York*

9

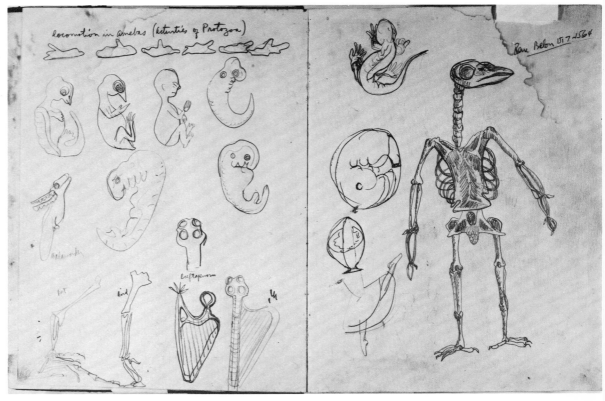

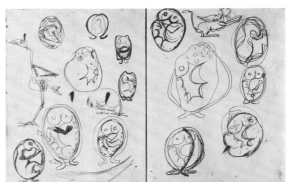

didn't speak French, he said, and besides, he heard he would have to address Picasso as *Maitre,* which he wasn't prepared to do."[32] Graham also introduced them to Jacques Lipchitz, but the meeting was not a success. "Cold. A great snob," Dehner remembers. (Ten years later, Lipchitz saw some of Smith's work in New York and admitted, "He is not without talent.")[33]

Smith's notebooks bear witness to his intense scrutiny of the old masters he was able to study in European museums. He was fascinated by technical details and devoted considerable time to noting the techniques and state of preservation of Northern Renaissance paintings.[34] When the couple spent the winter in Greece, he obtained permission to take samples of paint from sculpture at Olympia; he wanted to examine the remains of Greek polychromy under a microscope.[35] This kind of exhaustive study of anything which interested him seems typical of Smith, according to the evidence of the notebooks. There are pages of carefully drawn musical instruments, both real and invented,[36] along with names of early composers and copious notes from Aaron Copeland's *What to Listen for in Music* (and revealingly, the word "AUTODIDACT" in large letters).[37] There are drawings of protozoa,[38] studies of the locomotion of amoebas,[39] skeletons of prehistoric creatures, meticulous comparative studies of embryos and foetuses,[40] often accompanied by clippings and photographs relating to the subject. There are equally comprehensive notes on techniques of metal working, including smelting and welding, and on the properties of various metals and alloys.[41] It's an indication not only of the catholicity of Smith's sources, but of the voraciousness with which he consumed information and assimilated material, all of which he later transformed in his sculpture.

Other notes made during the European trip are equally revealing. It wasn't only the condition of Northern Renaissance pictures which absorbed his attention. He described Breughel's "surrealism,"[42] as he calls it, carefully noting fish in trees and other allusions to Flemish proverbs, without any sense of their metaphorical but down to earth meanings, and he rather gruesomely catalogued martyrdoms and tortures in other paintings. One entry reads:

> Realism — whipping — tortures of royalty on people — hangings — stretchings — choking with hot water — chopping of hands — recording of trials [illegible] the injustice recorded with sanctimonious faces henchmen of wealth.[43]

Not surprisingly, the Smiths' European year included a visit to the Soviet Union, whose politics and constructivist art, briefly officially supported, seemed to offer a provocative example to American artists living through the Depression. In a sense, the Smiths were too late, since a proclamation issued at the first All-Union Writers' Conference in 1934 had already announced the official jettisoning of the avant garde. Nevertheless, they were able to see the extraordinary collection of Matisses, early Cézannes, Picassos and their contemporaries at the Museum of Modern Western Art in Moscow.

The Smiths returned to the U.S. on July 4, 1936, and continued to alternate between Brooklyn Heights and Bolton Landing until they moved permanently to the farm in 1940. Smith worked there in relative isolation. The rather primitive, rigorous life at Bolton Landing appealed to him (and to Dehner), but they came to New York periodically to see art and friends, and remained in close touch with the city's small avant garde art world of the period.

Although Smith continued to paint and especially to draw as a way of generating and working out ideas, he was devoting himself more and more exclusively to sculpture by this time. He experimented with materials and approaches, making relief plaques, cast bronze and aluminum pieces, and welded iron and steel sculptures which often incorporated found objects. The works are uniformly small in scale, and explore a wide range of formal concerns, from swelling organic forms modelled and cast in bronze or iron, to attenuated constructions in sheet and rod.

It's relatively easy to identify the sources of many of these early works, whether sculptures or drawings. A group of reclining figures (Fig. 3) point to Giacometti's *Woman with her Throat Cut,* with slung forms and ringed trachea-like structures; the splayed flipper-hands of some figures suggest Picasso's bathers. Smith's chief source of information about the European moderns — particularly sculptors he admired — remained the illustrated magazine, so consequently, the few modernist works he *was* able to see first hand made an especially strong impression. The superb Gonzalez *Head* (1935-36) included in the Museum of Modern Art's 1936 exhibition, *Cubism and Abstract Art,* [44] is reflected quite directly in Smith's heads of 1938. An exhibition of the Spanish sculptor, Pablo Gargallo, at the Brummer Gallery in 1934, gave Smith an early opportunity to examine works he had probably seen in *Cahiers d'art,* and he appears to have been fascinated. He thought highly enough of the work to include a Gargallo (along with one of his own works) as illustrations for an article on modern sculpture that he published in *Architectural Record.* [45] The Spaniard's witty figures occupy a curious territory somewhere between sheet metal origami and Cubist construction, but in the absence of more challenging works they served as examples of Cubist ideas. Several Smiths of the late '30s show fairly direct influence. [46]

Giacometti's *The Palace at 4 AM* (Fig. 16) was a major work that Smith certainly knew well, both from magazine reproductions and from its exhibition at the Museum of Modern Art. [47] It's easy to document the powerful effect the sculpture had on Smith; the notion of using a building or interior as a theme seems to have interested him as much as the extreme linearity of the Giacometti. Yet while works like *Interior* (Fig. 9) and *Interior for Exterior* (Fig. 15) show an unequivocal debt to *The Palace at 4 AM,* they are equally remarkable for their evidence of Smith's individuality. The differences between the works are revealing.

The Giacometti sculpture is a frail, but logically constructed skeletal building, populated by forms utterly different from their surroundings. Part of the work's mystery is due to the extreme fragility of materials — thin slats of wood, glass, wire and string — and the precariousness of construction — insubstantial joints and suspended forms — all suggesting impermanence and imminent collapse. Smith appropriated Giacometti's imagery, but translated it into his own formal vocabulary, replacing the European refinement of *The Palace at 4 AM* with ad hoc transformations of unexpected materials. *Interior for Exterior,* for example, contains (among other things) something very much like a corkscrew, perhaps in lieu of the meticulously assembled "spine" of the Giacometti, while a flying pliers parodies the prehistoric bird of the earlier work. In Smith's hands, the delicately constructed, magic toy building becomes a rigid metal cage; light, swung forms become cast and forged masses.

Both Smith's and Giacometti's sculptures are linear, drawing-like, but *The Palace at 4 AM* is linear because Giacometti chose to make an equivalent for enclosure by reducing architectural forms to a metaphoric, schematic framework. Thinness is justified by structural logic. In Smith's sculptures, however, line functions independently of rational or descriptive needs. The central maze of *Interior,* for instance, cannot be interpreted literally as a diagram of a room and its contents. The lucid architecture of *The Palace* becomes, in Smith's language, irrational. We are given a suggestion of three-dimensional enclosure, not a definition: in short, Smith's responses to Giacometti's example are less elegant, more robust and more pictorial than the work which provoked them. This is all the more significant when we remember that Smith was able to see the actual Giacometti sculpture. We can't explain the pictorialism of *Interior* or *Interior for Exterior* by a supposed dependence on a two-dimensional reproduction; instead, we must acknowledge it as a deliberate choice.

1940s

The beginning of the 1940s saw Smith established at Bolton Landing with the start of a remarkably original provocative body of work. The advent of World War II and the United States' entry into the war, however, deeply affected his work as a sculptor. In spite of his profound anti-fascism, Smith was not enthusiastic about the possibility of being called up. In a letter to his dealer, Marian Willard, he wrote:

> I must keep out of an army camp. It would spoil my work and ruin me as well.[48]

Dorothy Dehner suggests that Smith was acutely aware of the violent side of his nature, and feared what licensed, organized violence might do to him.[49]

Smith made every effort to find a means of putting his abilities as a sculptor into the service of the war effort, offering "to make medallions to be awarded for extremely meritorious war production service in industry." The medals could be made "without metal priority and without affecting war effort machinery" and would be "of superior artistic quality."[50] As a final persuasive point, Smith wrote:

> I know workmen, their vision, because between college years I worked on Studebaker's production line and later on ship repair in Brooklyn harbor. Therefore I know what my art must be to reach them. My conception must be simple, concrete, presenting in terms of American history, events and things they know and respect in relation to our present efforts.[51]

In 1942, Smith also applied for a job in the design department of the American Locomotive Company, Schenactady, without success,[52] but was hired as a welder and remained for three years, until 1944. He lived in Schenectady and spent weekends at Bolton Landing, working on bronzes which often reflect themes of violence and destruction. Otherwise, he had little time for sculpture, and metal, in any case, was almost impossible to obtain. As a result, the drawings of this period are carefully worked out, surrogates for finished sculpture.

Smith managed to try his hand at carving, using power tools to cut stone at a tombstone works in Saratoga. *Sewing Machine* (Fig. 27) is one of the few works which remain of the series, since he was never entirely happy with marble as a medium. He wrote to Dorothy Dehner:

> Marble work goes slow. It's got to be slow otherwise it will chip off in the wrong places. However, I haven't got any metal or metal tools, not the ones I want, I mean . . .[53]

A few days later, he wrote:

> I had only a profile drawing to work from and as on the others, it was sufficient — I preferred it that way — but the slowness of mass removal foxed up somehow and now I'll have to reconceive and approach from a different concept. It's OK but it takes time to move from locomotives to aesthetics.[54]

At the Locomotive Works, Smith welded stainless steel armor plate on tanks. Although he was fond of drawing parallels between his jobs as machinist and welder, and his life as a sculptor, Dehner pointed out, in a letter to Lucille Corcos:

> It's lots different from acetylene welding also different from sculpture welding, because when you sculp [sic] you weld and then think, and when you weld, all you do is weld.[55]

Warlike images, or at least, images of brutality, are common in Smith's work of this period. A number of small bronzes deal unequivocally with themes of cannon-rape, while several *Spectres* savagely condemn political and social violence: *False Peace Spectre, Spectre of Profit* and *War Spectre,* for example. The most explicit of Smith's engagé sculptures, and the ones which would seem to have the most direct relation to the war, are the *Medals for Dishonor,* completed in 1939, after about three years' work.[56]

The medallions were conceived as an anti-war, anti-capitalist, anti-fascist protest, and were being circulated in a touring exhibition about the time the United States entered World War II. Smith was fearful that his anti-brutality images would be interpreted as isolationist, "America First propaganda or appeasement or Anti-American." He explained his intentions at length, when a reviewer in Minneapolis misunderstood the *Medals'* content.[57] When he wrote to the War Production Board, offering his skills as a sculptor, he was clearly worried that he might be rejected because of the *Medals for Dishonor:*

> This series hit the dishonorable and destructive elements of society. Certain elements, though true, might be interpreted as conflicting with the war effort. One fact I wish to restate — that my basic conception has always been anti-fascist and pro-democratic.[58]

When Smith left the American Locomotive Company, in 1944, and returned to full time sculpture making, he was able to realize, in three dimensions, the ideas he had explored as drawings while he lived in Schenectady. The marvelous *Home of the Welder* (Fig. 31) with its "wife made of locomotive parts" and the "millstone [which] hangs around his neck related to his job"[59] is an outstanding work — and perhaps the most obviously connected to the years at the locomotive factory. But the enormous variety, high quality and sheer numbers of the sculptures made in 1945 and 1946 are landmarks of Smith's early production. (Near-

ly a quarter of the sculptures in this exhibition date from this period.) Smith seemed free to try anything. There are pieces which are startling for their physical density and the density of their allusions, and others, no less complex, which present related themes with great economy and sparseness. They range from the tactile, modelled bronze of *Spectre Riding the Golden Ass* (Fig. 41) to the uncompromising two-dimensionality of *Steel Drawing I* (Fig. 42).

Smith exhibited regularly at the Willard Gallery during the '40s, and gradually acquired a small group of admirers. While he sold relatively few pieces, there were some significant purchases: the Museum of Modern Art acquired a 1938 *Head,* (Fig. 12) admittedly a

War Spectre, 1944
painted steel
36.8 x 57.5 x 17.2 cm
Collection of The Museum of Fine Arts, Houston

12

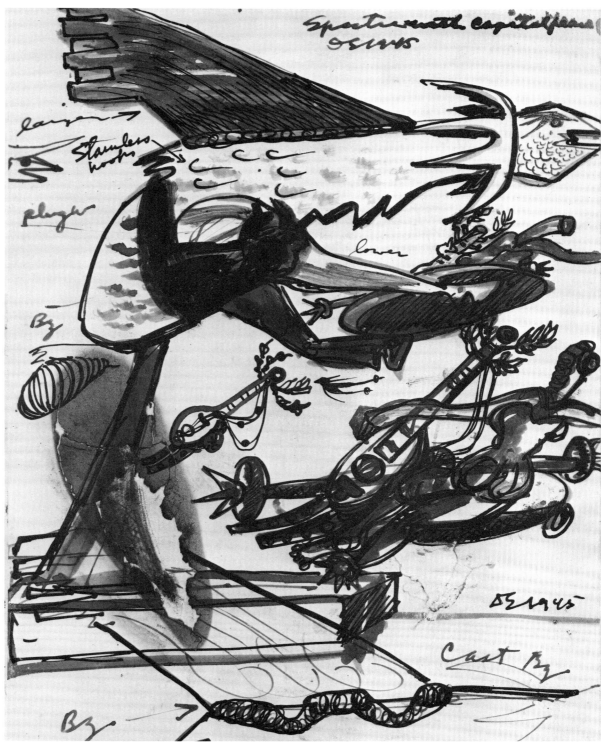

Spectre (recto) 1966.40
graphite and blue ink with black
and purple tempera
25.4 x 18.9 cm
Collection of the Fogg Art
Museum, Harvard University.
Gift of David Smith

modest work, in the '40s, while the Detroit Institute of Arts was given *Spectre Riding the Golden Ass* in 1947. Joseph Hirshhorn purchased several of Smith's early works, now in the Hirshhorn Museum and Sculpture Garden's collection. In 1946 some of the first sympathetic and enthusiastic reviews of Smith's work were written by Clement Greenberg, in *The Nation,* as early as 1943.[60] In 1944, Marian Willard's husband, Dan Johnson, introduced Greenberg to Smith, and a close friendship developed. Greenberg's criticism of Smith's sculpture remains some of the most perceptive and illuminating.

Smith's sculpture became increasingly inventive and ambitious during the second half of the '40s; it also became decreasingly specific, but it never lost the sense of highly charged *persona* which had characterized even the earlier work. By about 1950, however, the work shifted dramatically in scale, and at the same time, appeared far more abstract than most of what had come before. Because of this, Smith's sculpture after about 1951 can be seen as belonging to another phase of his evolution, yet there are characteristic images and formal concerns which can be traced throughout his career. It's this continuity which is perhaps most fascinating, since it points to what is peculiarly Smith's own. His work of the '30s and '40s, in addition to its intrinsic high quality, provides extraordinary insight into his preoccupations.

Themes of Content

Jurassic Bird, 1945
steel
64.5 x 89.5 x 19.1 cm
Private Collection

Despite its abstractness, the thematic obsessiveness of Smith's sculpture is unmistakable. Some images are more evident than others, even when they are presented in a distilled or disguised form. Rosalind Krauss has pointed out the persistance of types which she has termed Cannons, Totems, and Spectres,[61] while Smith himself declared that all his sculptures were female.[62] The allusions are usually clearer in the early works than in the later sculptures where Smith's recurring themes seem veiled or hidden. Dorothy Dehner has suggested that abstraction appealed to Smith as a means of concealment,[63] an approach which allowed him to make use of his most intimate emotions without entirely revealing himself.

Generally, the fierce intensity of Smith's sculpture is obvious from the first, hieratic welded heads. More specifically, themes of threat and violence noticeably pervade the sculptures of the '30s and '40s. In part, this could be justified as a reflection of the unrest of the times and the beginning of World War II, but Smith's notebooks and drawings document a deeper attraction to the brutal and the menacing. In addition to the catalogue of tortures in the Northern Renaissance paintings he saw in Europe, there are innumerable disturbing inclusions. In one sketchbook, Smith copies out a horrifying description of the atrocities of a 15th century sadist, in which a stripped and bound woman screams with pain as she gives birth and wolves devour her child.[64] He clipped and saved a magazine article about American soldiers at the front, circling a passage in which one G.I. described his desire to shoot pregnant German women.[65] Another sketchbook inclusion tells of a newborn child eaten by rats.[66]

The phallic cannons which appear in so many works — even, as Krauss has pointed out, as the mortar-like *Zigs* of the '60s — appear in countless notebook drawings, either straightforwardly as weapons, or as animate hybrid creatures, rather like Bosch's composite monsters.[67] There are cannon-snails, cannons with wings, or legs, or arms waving hatchets, cannons with phallic snouts, and innumerable variations. In a Goya-esque image, a seated cannon devours a figure;[68] elsewhere, cannon-phalluses attack female nudes. These images of nudes and rampant phallic artillery (Fig. 26) (like the photographs of heavy weapons with drawn additions, which accompany them)[69] are sometimes used by Smith quite literally as shorthand symbols for the brutality of war. A few small bronzes, such as this exhibition's *Atrocity* (Fig. 24), and some of the *Medals for Dishonor*, develop the cannon-rape theme explicitly.

Perhaps more serious, and certainly more suggestive, is a recurrent winged, birdlike phallic-cannon, which appears most obviously in a small bronze, *Ritual* (Fig. 25), and in various guises in *Head as a Still Life* (Fig. 18), *War Spectre, False Peace Spectre, Pillar of Sunday* (Fig. 34), *Jurassic Bird, Spectre of Mother* (Fig. 44), and *Royal Incubator* (Fig. 50) — among others. The image is sometimes triumphantly erect, sometimes suspended or limp. There's also a provocative series of notebook drawings, a sort of theme and variations on bird embryos which are gradually transformed into curled, foetal phallic-cannons.[70] There's an obvious similarity between Smith's drooping phallic gun and the limp snout of the polyp-like Franco figure in Picasso's anti-fascist cartoon, *The Dream and Lie of Franco.*[71] But where Picasso clearly means his creature's hideous proboscis to stand as an unequivocal metaphor for the repellant and the inhuman, Smith is less specific. He refuses to declare himself, preferring ambiguity, no matter how overt the reference.

The bird images, for example, which appear throughout Smith's early sculpture, are unmistakably avian, but evoke myriad responses in the viewer. They range from the springing winged phallus of *Roval Incubator,* to the skeleton of *Jurassic Bird,* to the jaunty oversized *Big Rooster* (Fig. 28), inviting speculation about flight, escape, "ruling the roost," even about evolution. Some of the spectres, especially the American eagle parody of *False Peace Spectre,* are birdlike, as well, while the notebooks include a pair of drawings labelled "small totems," which are, in fact, harpies: women with bird legs and wings — with wheels, like cannons.[72] In another context, *Pillar of Sunday,* Smith identified the winged form at the top as: "Bird found in Assyrian sculpture which was the bird that represented the soul that revisited the body," and called another birdlike figure: "Mother with two children in perambulator protected by her wings."[73] The same sculpture includes a "guitar form, meaning music as unity of chicken dinner and communion, which as a kid was one and the same."[74]

A similar association is made on the "platter" held by the *False Peace Spectre* in a drawing. Smith groups a guitar shaped like a female torso, a phallic lute sprouting laurel leaves, and a spiked double-ended mace, all supported by the bird-like *Spectre's* outthrust claw.

Chickens and roosters are frequent, and equivocal, images. The *Big Rooster,* whom Dorothy Dehner iden-

tifies as Smith himself, presides over an oddly classicizing farmyard with a round arch, Renaissance column and a relief image of hens on nesting boxes, while the sketchbooks contain a bizarre series of drawings of nude women eviscerating and dismembering plucked chickens.[75] As though to sum up the list of possible bird — or poultry — associations, Smith drew an extremely unprepossessing chicken as an illustration for the text: "When Plato identified man as a featherless animal on two legs, Diogenes plucked a cock and tossed it into the academy, saying, 'There is Plato's man'."[76] (And it should be noted that the Smiths raised chickens at Bolton Landing.)

Because of this deliberate ambiguity, this multiplicity of associations, it's obviously dangerous to draw too many conclusions about Smith's imagery. *Jurassic Bird,* for example, is a suggestive hierarchy of appar-

14

ently unrelated elements: a birdlike skeleton is suspended — "flown" — above a platform supporting two lively winged phallic-cannons, and in turn supported by coiling fish forms. An early drawing relating to the sculpture makes the skeleton into a boatlike object, with a mast rather like the mast in *Home of the Welder* (Fig. 31)[77]. The fish in the lower levels of the sculpture are extremely clear in the drawing. Another notebook entry itemizes "two fish, one lungfish" and a "foetus form,"[78] and in the same book, Smith pasted a clipping about icthyologists who revived a lungfish which had spent four years dormant in its container of dried mud.[79] Significantly, the fish in the early drawing for *Jurassic Bird* are given the distinctive limblike ventral fins of lungfish, and the resulting form is made to serve as an inverted approximation of the familiar winged cannon-phallus.

The notebooks and photographs found among the artist's papers also make it clear that Smith used a museum display of a skeleton of a prehistoric bird as a point of departure.[80] Dorothy Dehner remembers that they used to buy photographs from the Museum of Natural History.[81] Certainly the ingenious way the

bird-skeleton in the sculpture is suspended between vertical uprights suggests the mounting of a museum specimen. But despite his careful notes on the meaning and pronunciation of "jurassic" and a reminder, elsewhere, "stygosaur — reptilian — developed vertabrae ending at mezozoic,"[82] it's evident that Smith was more interested in the formal possibilities of superimposed images and strung, suspended bird/bone forms than in paleontological accuracy. (Elevated "skeletal" drawing occurs again in *Royal Bird* (Fig. 45) and later in *Australia,* 1951, while strung riblike forms recur in *Portrait of the Eagle's Keeper* (Fig. 49) and *Royal Incubator* (Fig. 50).) It's equally evident that while Smith was making some sort of personal metaphor for growth or hermetic transformation or preservation, the allusion is ultimately so private that it remains an overtone rather than a declaration.

Smith sometimes wrote accompanying texts for his sculpture, for exhibitions. But even when he was being most explanatory, he could be misleading, since it's clear that he intended no single meaning to be attached to any single image. One of the spectres, *Race for Survival,* is labelled a "capital(ist) monster" who holds something Smith identified as "the tied people carried in a spoon."[83] Yet in another context, he wrote of including "cast iron spoons, ladles, female objects . . ."[84] in a sculpture, as domestic attributes devoid of political meaning.

Smith's images then, are complex, serious visual puns, layered with meaning the way James Joyce's portmanteau words are. Smith admired Joyce greatly, and often alluded to *Finnegan's Wake* in relation to his own work. In an interview in 1964, Smith asked his questioner, Thomas Hess: "Do you know the Little Red Hen that scratched up a letter? Well, I'm always scratching up letters and that's one of the nice things about Joyce. There's part of Joyce in me all my life."[85] (As well as offering another general association with Smith's chicken images, Joyce's Little Red Hen, who scratched up a letter "you sent for me," provides a partial explanation for a curious drawing in one of the notebooks: a kneeling, humanized female chicken holds a sheet of paper in her mouth.)[86]

The dreamlike compression of multiple meanings in Smith's images is allied to his belief that the unconscious was "that region of the mind from which the artist derives his inspiration."[87] There can be no definite interpretation of his amalgamation of birds, guns, snails, embryos and phalluses, for example — nor should there be one — even, I would suggest, for the trained psychoanalyst. Smith's visual punning is probably not wholly conscious, but arises from the same source as his receptiveness to suggestions in the development of a sculpture, his alertness to the possibilities inherent in found objects, or his recognition of the overlapping characteristics of apparently unrelated objects. It serves to enrich his sculpture and make it more mysterious.[88]

His Cubist ancestors used visual puns as well, but they were limited to superficial physical similarities. A still life, for instance, might emphasize the likeness between the circular shapes of grapes, a bottle mouth and a wine glass, or a portrait might stress the equivalence of eyes, nostrils, knuckles and buttons. Compared to Smith's palimpsests of meaning, these Cubist puns seem lighthearted and playful; perhaps it would be more accurate to describe them as visual rhymes.

But despite Smith's consideration and exploitation of evocative associations, it's plain that formal con-

Notebook Drawings 3/642
Smith Papers, on deposit
Archives of American Art
Smithsonian Institution

siderations are as overwhelmingly important as the expression of emotion. Even one of Smith's most literally expressive (and most literally explained) images, the explicitly modelled bronze, *Spectre Riding the Golden Ass* (Fig. 41), probably has as much to do with aesthetic precedent as it does with an overt message. Smith described his supposed intentions in reply to a request from Franklin Page of the Detroit Institute of Arts when the museum received the sculpture:

> The *Spectre Riding the Golden Ass* came in my Spectre series, which related to the false values and evils of our civilization. This specifically related to the noises of war and evil trumpeted through the golden mouths of asses; that which is done for money knowingly or unknowingly. It relates to the means of communication that can be purchased for gold, and the false oversincerity which gold can purchase in radio, press and movies.
>
> Sometimes all mythology is condensed to point out present-day false values, as a dream logically can do. I am interested in the recurring myth, from prehistoric Egypt to the present day. I read all the cuneiform translations I can find, and I like the mythology of all cultures, the analyses of it, and the analysis of man, why he makes the reoccuring myth and justifying evil.
>
> Of course, none of this was necessarily as conscious as that when I made the sculpture. It carries about as much in the title as I had in conscious direction. It says that a vulgar broken winged spectre blows a trumpet through the mouth of a broken-down but golden ass, loud brass and false noises.[89]

Smith's sources for this disturbing image are characteristically varied. The spectre who stands on the ass' back is the familiar Smith-Bosch animated hybrid, with a thick phallic head and torso, wings, human legs ending in frog-like feet, and ambiguous testicle/

Aquamanile, 13th Century
German metalwork
bronze
36.2 x 35.6 cm
Collection of the
Metropolitan Museum of Art,
New York

breasts. (Inexplicably, the figure wears something rather like a pair of boxer shorts.) The head of the ass, with its open mouth, flaring nostrils and stretched ears, owes a great deal to the heads of Picasso's tortured horses, while the kneeling swaybacked pose of the creature is almost identical to that of the gored horses in the drawings which relate to *Guernica*.[90] The image of a horrifying mounted figure has precedents, too, in the riders of *The Dream and Lie of Franco*, while one of Smith's notebook sketches of

the early '40s shows an odd lion-like creature, ridden by a crowned female figure.[91]

The beast's head and neck are reduced to the familiar phallic cannon, held (or supported) by the rider's hand, while a vaguely Egyptian "offering table" construction protrudes from the back. A thirteenth century acquamanile in the collection of the Metropolitan Museum offers a striking parallel; the alterations and elisions of the notebook drawing seem consistent with Smith's usual transformations.

Perhaps the most elusive prefiguration of *Spectre Riding the Golden Ass* is William Blake's engraving *O! How I dreamt of Things Impossible,* of 1796. The work was included in the Museum of Modern Art's exhibition, *Fantastic Art, Dada, Surrealism,* where Smith must have seen it. (It was also reproduced in the catalogue.)[92] The flying horse of Blake's fantasy spouts fire from his nostrils and bears two riders. The disposition of flames and rein leads to an effect similar to the piercing of the ass' head by the Spectre's trumpet. The disparity of sources and the freedom with which Smith assimilated them seems typical.

But if Spectre *Riding the Golden Ass* seems characteristic of Smith's early engagé works in its imagery, political allusions and sources, it also points the way to later, more abstract works. Like many of Smith's sculptures, the *Spectre* is essentially two dimensional. Even though it is realized in the round and solidly modelled, the two side views are clearly dominant, while the head-on and tail-on views of the beast are definitely subordinate.

From head on, Smith forces the visual equivalence of the straining ears of the ass and the upcurved wings of the spectre, the phallus tip and the ass' mouth and horn. These likenesses are reinforced by the insistently repeated texture of wings, mane, tail and hair on the ass' legs. But it is the open caging of forms, the complex play of spectre, horn, legs, tail and base, all surrounding and activating relatively large sections of space, which seems most characteristic of Smith. Even the open mouth of the ass, with its projecting tongue and transfixing horn, echos in miniature the structure of the whole. For all its literalness, and for all the naturalism of its forms, it's not an overstatement to say that even *Spectre Riding the Golden Ass* anticipates Smith's sparser, more abstract, drawing-like sculpture.

Themes of Structure

However compelling the thematic content of Smith's sculpture, it is obvious that formal constants of even greater power reverberate through his work. It's possible to identify recurrent habits of construction, just as it's possible to identify recurrent images. We recognize a characteristic vocabulary of structures: cages, elevated "monstrances," and enclosures, among others. But Smith's sculptural syntax exists almost independently of specific content, or rather, his formal types resist identification with individual themes. Even when he seems to have arrived at a particular configuration by means of a particular image, he easily disassociates his discovery from whatever provoked it, and develops its implicit possibilities at some other scale or in some other context.

The cage recurs in many guises. In the '30s, it often seems to have a lingering connection with scaffolding or enclosure, as in *Interior* (Fig. 9) or *Interior for Exterior* (Fig. 15), at the same time that it exists as "pure" drawing. But the motif quickly loses these associations. If the notion of sculpture as a linear enclosure originally owed anything to Giacometti's *The Palace at 4 AM* (Fig. 16), Smith managed to make the idea his own and put it into the service of his own formal needs, divorced from any architectural connections. It persists in intricate multiple groupings, such as *Bathers* (Fig. 20), in elevated structures such as *Maiden's Dream* (Fig. 46) and *Jurassic Bird,* in the solemn *Portrait of the Eagle's Keeper* (Fig. 49), even in the spare, open *Blackburn* (Fig. 54). In the '30s and '40s, caging seems related to Smith's desire to acknowledge mass without resorting to solid forms, but later, in the superb, large scale drawing-sculptures of the '50s, such as *Hudson River Landscape* and *The Banquet,* the cage is flattened, allowed — or forced — to become more completely optical and pictorial.

Similarly, Smith's habit of elevating his sculptures by setting them on undisguised legs or "putting them on a stick," seems at first to have something to do with the figure. (Man's normal upright posture, after all, offers automatic solutions to sculptural problems of raising mass and relating it to the base.) In his early heads and works like *Head as a Still Life* (Fig. 18), he relied on these figurative associations to justify structural requirements and to provide a basis for formal invention. A linear volume, held on a slender support, became an equivalent for head and neck or sometimes, for torso and legs. In other works of the '30s and '40s, Smith used the same formal device in works which didn't allude directly to the figure, but profited from the sense of confrontation which results from the figurative associations of the elevated mass. In *Construction on a Fulcrum* (Fig. 5) and *Widow's Lament* (Fig. 21), to name just a few, forms are hoisted up to present them to view like the relics in a liturgical monstrance. In *Pillar of Sunday* (Fig. 34) and *Blackburn* (Fig. 54), the vertical support itself becomes more dominant, a totemic structure which serves to organize and to display a series of physically detached but psychologically related images. Yet even here, in spite of the neutrality of the supporting structure, a vaguely figurative presence remains, since our strong sense of our own bodies makes us read upright shapes and forms as body-like, and to experience deviations from uprightness in terms of physical gestures. In the '50s and '60s, Smith continued to rely on this kind of humanoid verticality, and on the unignorable presence of the object on a stick, to animate even his most abstract constructions.

In other works of the '30s and '40s, especially *Home of the Welder* (Fig. 31) and *Reliquary House* (Fig. 37), rationally constructed, simple containers substitute for the vertical "monstrance" as a means of presenting suggestive, disparate forms. In these, figurative

Maiden's Dream, 1947-48
bronze
68.6 x 49.5 x 50.8 cm
Collection of The Estate of David Smith
Courtesy of M. Knoedler and Co., New York

Head as a Still Life, 1940
cast iron and bronze
39.4 x 44.5 x 19.7 cm
Collection of The Estate of David Smith
Courtesy of M. Knoedler and Co., New York

Widow's Lament, 1942   *K 150*
forged and fabricated steel
and bronze
34.3 x 50.8 x 16.8 cm,
on base 6.4 x 20.3 x 12.7 cm
Private Collection

associations are replaced by the literal presence of the *made,* inanimate object, while the enigmatic objects placed within the box-like structures (like the miniature forms buried in the square tubes of *Widow's Lament*) suggest an allusion to hermetic enclosure and transformation, a common theme among Smith's colleagues of the period.[93]

Reliquary House has been thoroughly anatomized and its relation to a medieval reliquary and a 17th century illustration of the influence of the moon on women seems clear enough.[94] *Home of the Welder,* in general concept, and because of its tight, room-like compartments — and the way we look down into them — suggests a link with the Metropolitan Museum's remarkable collection of Egyptian building models, complete with gardens, furnishings and figures, intended to perpetuate everyday life for the owner of the tomb to which they were consigned. (Since Smith conceived the piece while working as a welder at the American Locomotive Company in Schenectady and living in furnished rooms, the connection may be psychological as well as formal.) *Royal Incubator* (Fig. 50) extends the theme of neutral enclosure to a less specific structure; while the idea of hermetic transformation is implicit in the central foetal form and the perched cannon/bird above, literal enclosure has itself been transformed into a suggestive pictorial framework.

In the '30s and '40s, whether Smith dealt with "cages," "monstrances" or neutral enclosures, he fre-

quently appeared to have conceived of the large structure of his sculpture primarily as an untraditional means of supporting and unifying groups of composite glyphs. It's an approach not unlike that of his friend Adolph Gottlieb, whose Pictographs of the 1940s are based on a schematic grid which serves to organize, but not contain, a whole lexicon of allusive drawn and painted forms. Like Smith's conflated images, Gottlieb's, too, call forth a great number of associations which overlap, reinforce and cancel one another.

Royal Incubator, 1949
steel, bronze, silver
94 x 97.5 x 25.1 cm
Collection of
Mr. and Mrs. C. Bagley Wright

But where Gottlieb's glyphs are disembodied drawn signs which can expand across the boundaries of the grid, Smith's are self-contained, often solid (cast) forms. Like the modelled and cast sculptures of the period — *Spectre Riding the Golden Ass* (Fig. 41), *Atrocity* (Fig. 24), *Perfidious Albion* (Fig. 36) and their fellows — the glyphs are not optical, pictorial images, but discrete *things,* usually quite complex and realized in the round: fetish-like. However disguised and ambiguous, these forms often seem to be the carriers of the symbolic, allusive content of the sculptures.[95] In Smith's early works, a variety of linear structures display or enclose the glyphs, without overwhelming them. But by the late '40s, when Smith's sculpture begins to increase in scale, these relatively neutral "supports" become more expressive and dominant, as in *Royal Incubator* (Fig. 50) or *Blackburn* (Fig. 54). In the sculptures of the '50s and '60s, the glyphs are either completely subsumed by the larger structure, or disappear entirely. No matter how simplified the sculpture, it seems to exist entirely for its own sake, not as a scaffold for references. Yet these larger structures are neither neutral nor arbitrary; they, in turn, take on the composite, allusive qualities of the glyphs. Instead of totemic supports for small "units of meaning," we are confronted by large hieratic constructions which seem at once unlike anything familiar or preexisting, and charged with allusive overtones.

In addition to Smith's repeated habits of construction, we recognize more idiosyncratic constants, characteristics which, in part, make his sculpture hard to perceive and sometimes, hard to like. From our present vantage point, we are no longer startled by his use of non-art materials. (We're more likely to be surprised when he uses bronze.) But the oddness of Smith's forms, the intensity of his imagery, and the vernacular casualness with which he attacks formal issues, still challenge us. Smith makes our assumptions of good taste irrelevant, but this is not the only difficulty. The sculptures are spatially ambiguous and their genesis seems elusive. We may find a work arresting and disturbing, but the logic of its conception and evolution is not immediately apparent.

It's true that in many sculptures of the '30s this is less obvious, since they begin with relatively conventional conceptions — heads, reclining figures, standing figures — no matter how unexpected their shapes and forms. But they are no less elusive.

The collaged constructions Smith made in 1933, such as *Agricola Head* (Fig. 1) and *Saw Head* (Fig. 2), may seem to be fairly straightforward derivations of Cubist precedents, but even at this early date, Smith transformed his found objects in a way which completely subverts the role such objects played in the work of his predecessors. The ball fringe and absinth spoon of Picasso's constructions, like the oil cloth patterns and newspapers of the collages, were meant to declare themselves frankly as what they were, not to disappear into a new whole. By calling attention to another, more familiar world of objects, these inclusions were intended to make the invented *made* forms of other elements seem more extraordinary and, at the same time, more convincing as a self-contained alternative to actuality. The ambiguity of the actual objects, the flux between the real and the made, are a great part of the pleasure of these constructions. (It's no accident that Picasso always adhered to the proper size of the images he built: the guitars, the *Glass of Absinth* and the still life constructions are all life size,

19

while the oval of the seminal *Still Life with Chair Caning* of 1912, approximates the size and shape of the chair seat which the caning evokes.) Smith's shears and saw blade, however, are made to take their places discreetly in a formal whole, completely subservient to the head which they suggest. (Picasso, too, would do this, in his *Colander Head.*) Smith, paradoxically, disembodies the found elements in his early works, turning them into drawing, instead of massing them to describe a volume, as Picasso often did, or Gonzalez, in works such as *Head, called the Tunnel.*

Smith rarely again used found objects quite as playfully or as literally as he did in *Saw Head* the exceptions are, of course, the *Voltri* "workbenches," *XVI* and *XIX.* But in his best works, found objects, like forged or cast elements, are exploited for their shapes and gestures as drawing, and are completely subsumed by the whole. When the origins of the object remain too recognizable, the work suffers. Success, in fact, often depends upon Smith's ability to dema-

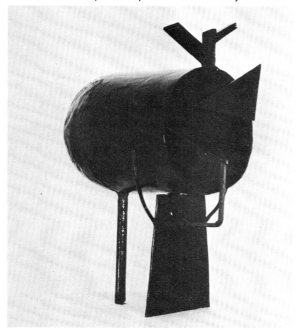

Julio Gonzalez
Head called "The Tunnel", 1933
bronze
46.4 cm high
Private Collection

Sawhead, 1933
iron, painted orange
47 x 30.5 x 21 cm
Collection of The Estate of David Smith
Courtesy of M. Knoedler and Co., New York

terialize the found object and force it to take its place in a spatially elusive structure.

Obviously, it is part of the legacy of Cubist collage to make sculpture by physically taking an assortment of things and sticking them together to make a new kind of object. But Smith's approach goes beyond a literal assembly of pre-existing parts to an even more fundamental idea of Cubism. Many of his sculptures deal with notions of collaging perceptions, not things. They seem the result of Smith's having aggressively appropriated a great variety of pictorial elements and conflating them into a single structure. It's not just a question of amalgamating several views of the same object, as Cubist painters often did.

Billiard Player Construction (Fig. 6), for example, is a powerful unit which can be analyzed as a fusion of the surface of a pool table and the players. The sculpture's development is documented by Smith's notebooks and drawings, and by his carefully saved clipping of a *Life* picture story about Willy Hoppe.[96] The subject has firm basis in Smith's everyday experience as well; in the early '30s, he and his neighbor, Adolph Gottlieb frequently shot pool together in local Brooklyn Heights billiard parlors.[97] But the sculpture is anything but literal. Smith not only flattened and truncated the central figure, turning him into a triangular shape joined to the playing surface of the table, but he telescoped space, linking disjointed forms into single planes.

The odd pierced shape in the lower part of the sculpture, rather like the stylized f-hole on a Cubist violin, resolves itself, for example, with the help of the drawings, as billiard balls and/or a player's hand, disembodied, flattened, and turned into a negative arabesque. Similarly, the pierced "heads" of the upright plane cannot be assigned any particular place in space. From the "front" of the sculpture, it is possible to read them (it) as the head of the player, or of more distant figures, or simply as a kind of counterpoint to other linear elements in the work. Yet the other side of the sculpture has a peculiar arrangement of horizontal bands which seem to delineate two figures, an impression reinforced by an astonishing painted passage which continues, on a flat plane, the open shapes above, implying even greater spatial ambiguity between near and far forms than is apparent from the "front."

The sculpture seems the result of Smith's laying claim to a great many forms from his surroundings and compressing them into new relationships which owe little to their original scale or their original disposition in space. (Drawings for *Billiard Player Construction* (Fig. 7,8), in fact, show several conjoined and interlocked figures, while references to the interior of the poolroom are as dominant as the players.) The same kind of willful fusion informs such sculptures as *Sewing Machine* (Fig. 27), which despite its vaguely Mayan presence, is decipherable as a woman sewing.[98] The figure is implied only by allusions to a hand and a head, detached from logical context and absorbed into the shape of the machine.

This kind of amalgamating, all-inclusive vision is a painter's habit. As long as any reference to visible reality remained, it was part of the painter's task to distill information about his surroundings into a lucid formal whole. The random variety of the perceivable world had to be organized and absorbed into a two-dimensional surface. Free standing sculpture, on the

20

other hand, proceeded from an entirely different premise. The traditional figurative monolith stamped itself out as unlike its surroundings, instead of absorbing those surroundings into itself. It displaced space, establishing its own internal rules of distance and measurement by the placement of spatially distinct, discrete parts. Because it referred to familiar visible reality, usually to the human figure, its singleness and wholeness were immediately comprehensible.

Smith's sculpture declares its self-sufficiency by looking like nothing except itself, but at the same time, its individuality results from a willful bringing together of disparate elements, not by a rejection of its surroundings. It's as though, in order to avoid conventional sculptural relationships dictated by existing forms, Smith tried to encompass everything within range of his sight. It's especially clear in his drawings, from the '30s to the end of his life: space is elided; near

Billiard Player Construction, 1937
iron and encaustic
43.8 x 42.1 x 16.2 cm
Collection of
Dr. and Mrs. A.E. Kahn, New York

Notebook Drawing 4/75
Smith Papers, on deposit
Archives of American Art
Smithsonian Institution

and far elements are forced into the same plane; individual solids dissolve into arrangements of lines.

A 1934 drawing, *The artist photographing a sculpture* (Fig. 10), marries the figure, his equipment, the sculpture, its support and the paraphenalia of the room, in an image close to the tangled center of the 1937 sculpture, *Interior* (Fig. 9). A 1949 ink study of a standing nude gives equal weight to the model, the stool on which she leans, some books and a distant view through a window. Like Matisse, Smith awards equal significance to each part of his image, diffusing attention throughout the drawing, but instead of simply spreading elements across the page, he links them, despite their inconsistencies of scale, as though to make it clear that he thinks of them as a potential sculptural object. Yet it is a sculptural object quite

Sewing Machine, 1943
stone on wood base
31.1 x 57.2 x 6.7 cm
Courtesy of the André Emmerich Gallery

unlike the space displacing monolith, since it is made up of tenuously related parts and penetrated by surrounding space.

Smith could transform individual objects in similar ways. A notebook drawing of a bizarre, apparently abstract image eventually reveals itself as a dancer, with limbs not only extended, but fused one to another. The image may have something to do with a Picasso figure-type of the late '20s and early '30s, a flattened starfish silhouette with head, arms and legs all radiating from a central point. Picasso's figures make only a casual reference to normal anatomy, but face, hands and feet are usually indicated, as if to insure recognition that it *is* a human form. Smith's dancer is disguised to the point of becoming an independent abstract object, a self-sufficient construction of continuous loops and arcs.[99]

But no matter how purely formal this physical asso-

ciation of disparate units may be, it is also related to Smith's use of visual puns. The curious hybrid, *Table Torso* (Fig. 23), like the furnishings of *Interior*, probably derives from Smith's ordinary experience of sculptural forms set upon improvised supports. Giacometti, too, made sculpture about tables with things on them, and Smith returned several times to the motif, which culminates, perhaps, in the "workbench" *Voltri X* and *Voltri XIX* of 1962. The fused woman-table also persists: *Voltri Bolton XXIII,* 1963, for example, can be read as both a vertical female figure and as a table with still life. *Table Torso,* with its strange swaybacked figure and collapsing plant-like base, is itself a kind of inversion of the torso-based table of *Home of the Welder* (Fig. 31), in which a female form supports a plant form.[100]

Smith's collaging of spatially distinct elements leads either to sculpture of extraordinary complexity or of deceptive simplicity. In bringing discontinuous things into unexpected proximity, Smith could compress them into a single plane, as in *Sewing Machine* (Fig.

21

27) and *Steel Drawing I* (Fig. 42), or disperse them in apparently illogical ways, as in *Landscape with Strata* (Fig. 43). In works like *Pillar of Sunday* (Fig. 34) and *Home of the Welder* (Fig. 31), he substituted psychological discontinuousness for physical, arranging discrete units charged with ambiguous meanings, on relatively coherent frameworks. In any case, he refused to adhere to conventional sculptural relationships when he assembled his works; ideas of a single preferred view or of anticipated transitions in the round, are not part of Smith's vocabulary.

The 1945 piece, *Steel Drawing I,* anticipates later works in which two-dimensional shapes and configurations take over completely and, as a result, the least venture away from the dominant plane becomes enormously important. For its date, the work is remarkable for its literal translation of pictorial, two-dimensional concerns into a free standing sculptural object. We are presented with an unequivocally flat sheet of metal, set upright and minimally shaped. The pierced drawing, a Picasso-inspired studio interior, with artist, easel and reclining model, is as spatially compressed and ambiguous as the early "artist photographing" drawing, yet an illusion of three-dimensional depth is suggested by the explicit, albeit schematic, rendering of the room's perspective. The sculpture can, of course, be read in many ways, but the optical play between literal flatness and implied space is an important part of its success. Since the drawing is cut through the sheet, and since end views are virtually non-existent, each side of the sculpture presents the same faintly illusionistic image, compounding the already potent spatial ambiguity. It's not like a relief, in which pictorial illusion suggests three-dimensional mass and space. The fact of Smith's pierced drawing serves to emphasize the two-sidedness and physicality of the piece; the latent illusion of the image serves to disembody and to dissolve it.

However pictorial the early sculpture may be, the best pieces (like much of the best mature work) are strongly marked by powerfully clear sculptural articulation, no matter how much the whole image may depend upon optical connections and no matter how much it may result from visual amalgamation. Transitions from part to part are always decisive and lucid. It's not simply a result of an additive constructed method. Even in predominantly two-dimensional images, such as *Head as a Still Life* (Fig. 18) or *Widow's Lament* (Fig. 21), forms are butted together forthrightly; changes of direction or plane, no matter how subtle, are declared with the emphasis of a theatrical gesture. The notched shape of *Steel Drawing I,* for example, serves to affirm that the piece *is* a freestanding piece of sculpture, not just a neutral ground for drawing.

Whether he deals with relatively simple, relatively identifiable images, such as the early heads or the humanoid *Perfidious Albion* (Fig. 36), or with enigmatic, more abstract constructions, Smith differentiates each side of the work very clearly, just as he obviously expresses the juncture of part to part. In *Sewing Machine,* which offers a precedent for *Steel Drawing I*'s extreme two-dimensionality, partly because of its tombstone origins, there is a lingering allusion to front and back, implied by hair and eye pattern, but even here, he characteristically refuses to accord greater importance to either, and forces end views to be as different from front and back as front and back are from each other. In *Perfidious Albion,*

where the emphatic torso shape should permit us to predict the parts of the sculpture we cannot see, simply because of our familiarity with the human form, Smith confounds this expectation by marking each side of the "figure" with anatomically implausible reliefs, each totally different. As a result, it is almost impossible to anticipate the rest of the sculpture from any one view, a characteristic which remains constant throughout Smith's work, no matter how linear or complex the piece. There are exceptions, of course, in which symmetry — and slight variations from symmetry — are important, but more typically, the sculpture is different from each point of view, making even the most "legible" piece appear surprising and radically inventive.

It's as though Smith retained a potent sense of the individual perceptions which may have generated the sculpture at the same time that he denied the possibility of reconstructing them as an easily perceived unit. This is particularly true of the landscape sculptures of the '40s, such as *Landscape with Strata*. Rosalind Krauss has attributed the elusiveness of these sculptures to an "absence of core," that is, Smith's apparent freedom from the notion of a preconceived coherent mass as the genesis of his sculpture.[101] She points out, in support of this thesis, that the landscape elements of *Landscape with Strata* (Fig. 43) are intelligible from just one point of view.[102] From any other aspect, the piece can be seen only as a fairly arbitrary, if internally logical, construction. But this is equally true of Gonzalez's linear figures, which coalesce into explicit images from one view and dissolve into lively assortments of arcs and rods from any other. It's simply a characteristic of allusive linear sculpture: the image is usually obscure, except from a single point of view, unless it is turned into a "cage" inflected in response to all conceivable viewpoints, or the sculptor literally reconstructs three-dimensional equivalents for the generating object. Admittedly, Smith exaggerates the differences between points of view by treating each side of the sculpture as an almost independent composition and by seeming to ignore end views, but the unpredictable quality of his structures is not so much a coefficient of "absence of core" as of Smith's refusal to restrict himself to a single generating object.

When he does limit himself, as in the early heads, the component figures of more complex groups, or works such as *Perfidious Albion*, the result is relatively solid and comprehensible. When he gives full play to his ability to amalgamate, in a pictorial sense, it leads to explorations of remarkable themes — landscapes and interiors — which have precedents neither in traditional sculpture nor in construction. It could be argued, too, that Smith's desire to avoid sculptural precedents (as well as his relative unfamiliarity with them, at the beginning of his career) led him to themes which seemed antithetical to conventional notions of what sculpture could be. Since, for example, Picasso had amply demonstrated that still life could be as challenging a basis for sculpture as it was for painting, it's interesting to note that Smith appears to have avoided the motif, as a point of departure for three-dimensional construction. A few sculptures of the '30s are termed "heads as still life," but have no relation to Cubist prototypes. When Smith does attack as a theme, in the *Voltri* "workbenches" it is in his own, curiously vernacular mode, in terms of robust workmen's tools, not traditional studio props.

The Mechanics

Smith's formal inventiveness is intimately bound up with his technical ability, so much so that it's impossible to separate medium, method, and form, or even to speculate about which determined which. The meticulous notes about metalworking techniques and the properties of alloys, in an early notebook, are testimony to his fascination with the most basic aspects of his chosen method, while the article apparently based on these notes, published in *Architectural Record,*[103] treats almost exclusively of this aspect of sculpture making. "Sculpture; Art Forms in Architecture — New Techniques Affect Both" was written, Smith says, to summarize the new means available to the 20th century artist:

> . . . the thing that differentiates modern sculpture from all its predecessors is its *means* of achieving these aesthetic standards. Never before have the sculptors had so rich and varied a selection of materials, tools and techniques with which to work.[104]

Smith certainly didn't shy away from using whatever combination of materials or methods he felt he needed to achieve particular formal ends. In the '30s and '40s, he often radically varied components and techniques within the same work, according to the demands of surface or shape or drawing. A single piece may contain forged iron rods, steel planes and sheets, cast bronze biomorphic forms and an assortment of (altered) found objects.

This variety of materials contributes to changes of color, as well as of surface and form, from part to part. Smith seems to have liked these variations and sometimes exaggerated them with paint and patination; there are even a few early works in which each element is given a different color.[105]

Unlike many of his successors, Smith rarely used color as a means of cancelling disparities or of disembodying the substance of a work. Instead, he found ways of affirming differences of form and surface, as in the play of bronze glyphs and the dull, darker "container" in *Reliquary House,* or the red rubbed paint and greenish bronze patina of *Royal Incubator. Pillar of Sunday* is a rather unusual instance of Smith's choosing an unexpected, non-metallic color and applying it to the entire work, but because of its strong totemic structure, the piece is already possessed of a powerful unity; the single color simply asserts an essential property of the sculpture. In many painted works, Smith's characteristic brushy application functions as texture as much as color, setting up yet another distinction of part to part.

Polychromy, in the early works, never assumes the almost autonomous role it plays in Smith's later sculptures, yet from the article in *Architectural Record,* where he itemizes the colors inherent in various oxides and alloys, it's clear that he conceived of color as an essential part of sculpture, and one which could, theoretically, at least, be completely integrated with materials. The fact that Smith seemed to succeed best when he kept color variation very subtle, or made it subordinate to other aspects of the work, makes his preoccupation with the idea no less important.

The multiplicity of materials, colors and textures in Smith's early sculpture is, in a sense, both a legacy of his thinking as a painter and a natural extension of his uninhibited approach to collage. The desire to include steel, iron, silver and cast bronze in a single work, after all, isn't very different from the all-inclusive, amalgamating vision which makes Smith force together spatially disparate elements, in both drawings and sculpture. It seems inevitable, too, that in addition to assimilating (or improvising from) a wide range of existing forms, he would manufacture his own objects for inclusion.

Each material is treated so distinctively and so appropriately that Smith's sensitivity to the properties of metals becomes obvious. Steel's tensile strength is exhibited in thin papery planes and slender rods; iron is forged into painfully worked bars or cast in smooth solids; bronze records the marks of the modeller's hand in complex organic forms; found objects are divorced from function and used only for their shapes and forms. It's impossible to say whether the shape of a piece of steel or a farm implement dictated the final configuration of a sculpture, or whether Smith searched his stock for particular elements demanded by the work in hand,[106] but the prefabricated cast forms suggest, if not a fair amount of advance planning, at least a notable degree of meticulousness and concern for craft. Yet the cast portions of even the most complex sculptures seem to have been made in response to the specific requirements of the piece, as it evolved.

Smith insisted that his work was not premeditated, despite the evidence of drawings and notebooks that he explored ideas and forms quite thoroughly before starting to weld. But the sculptures are so unpredictable and their logic is so elusive, that it is tempting to regard them as spontaneous improvisations — plastic free associations. Smith explained the process:

> When I begin a sculpture, I am not always sure how it is going to end. In a way, it has a relationship to the work before, it is in continuity to the previous work — it often holds a promise or gesture towards the one to follow. I do not often follow its path from a previously conceived drawing. If I have a strong feeling about its start, I do not need to know its end, the battle for solution is the most important . . . Sometimes when I start a sculpture, I begin with only a realized part, the rest is travel to be unfolded much in the order of a dream.[107]

The drawings which relate to *Big Rooster* (Fig. 28) help explain this seeming contradiction. All the components of the sculpture are visible in the sketches, the cast of characters assembled: the rooster, the improbable Renaissance arch, the tractor, the sawtooth hen shape, and the hens on nesting boxes are all present and loosely grouped. There's even an odd dancing chicken who looks like a parody of some of the Boas Dancing School studies. But the final configuration of the sculpture was obviously arrived at in the course of working. Nothing in the drawings anticipates the taut splay of sawtooth to column, or the willful wrenchings of scale from towering rooster to miniature tractor to peculiarly diminished arch. These are all sculptural notions developed and expressed in the course of working in metal, in three dimensions. The drawings indicate only the individual images which preoccupied Smith, not the structure he would build with them.

Afterword

Time and two generations of heirs to Smith's new tradition of sculpture have not lessened the impact of his work. It remains inexpressibly modern and challenging, even disturbing. Paradoxically, it seems to combine unquestioning, powerful expressiveness, achieved at whatever cost, with tough-minded formal development. It's as though Smith worked with two apparently contradictory attitudes: on the one hand, he appears to have been dispassionately alert to possibilities which arose in the course of working, and on the other, intensely concerned with the invention — or discovery — of personal metaphorical images. He could be uncritical of his own production, not in the sense of being easily satisfied, but in insisting on the significance of everything he made as the declaration of a particular, special, individual. In any case, he disliked critical distinctions:

> The works you see are segments of my work life. If you prefer one work over another, it is your privilege, but it does not interest me. The work is a statement of identity, it comes from a stream, it is related to my past works, the three or four works in process and the work yet to come.[108]

Smith would have been 75 in 1981. His death at the age of 59 deprived us of what promised to be some of his most remarkable and most abstract sculpture. But we can only speculate about what might have followed the *Cubi*. There is no doubt about the quality or importance of Smith's early work. It is extraordinary for its evocative imagery, for its formal inventiveness, and for the insight it offers into what was to come.

References

Notes:

AAA citations refer to the David Smith Papers, or other collections on microfilm, in the Archives of American Art, Smithsonian Institution; the first figure is the roll number, the second is the frame number. Krauss numbers refer to the catalogue raisonné, *The Sculpture of David Smith.*

1. *American Art at Mid-Century, The Subjects of the Artist,* opening exhibition of the East Wing of the National Gallery, Washington, D.C., June 1, 1978 - January 14, 1979.
2. David Smith, interviewed by David Sylvester of the British Broadcasting Corporation, June 16, 1961; published in *Living Arts,* April 1964. Reprinted in *David Smith,* edited by Garnett McCoy, Praeger, New York and Washington, 1973, p. 174.
3. Smith, Sylvester interview, McCoy, p. 174.
4. David Smith, paper delivered at the Museum of Modern Art symposium, *The New Sculpture,* February 21, 1952. Reprinted, McCoy, p. 82.
5. Smith, Sylvester interview, McCoy, p. 172.
6. Paul Cummings, *David Smith: The Drawings,* Whitney Museum of American Art, New York, 1979, p. 11. For complete annotated chronology and biography, see "Chronology," pp. 39-43.
7. David Smith, autobiography (to 1947) written about 1950, reprinted in *David Smith on David Smith,* edited by Cleve Gray; Holt, Rinehart and Winston, New York, 1978, p. 24.
8. Smith, *The New Sculpture* paper, McCoy, p. 82.
9. Dorothy Dehner, in conversation, spring 1978.
10. David Smith, letter to Dorothy Dehner, June 1944, in Ms. Dehner's possession.
11. Graham's real name was Ivan Dabrowsky. He claimed to have chosen "Graham" because it resembled his mother's name written in Cyrillic characters. See Hayden Herrera, "John Graham, Modernist Turns Magus," *Arts* magazine, Vol. 51, October 1976, pp. 100-105.
12. Dorothy Dehner says that seeing John Graham's collection of African sculpture, in the late 1920s, was the Smiths' introduction to Negro art as something other than an "ethnic curiosity." Previously, they had seen it only in the Museum of Natural History. The Museum of Modern Art's large exhibition of African sculpture did not take place until 1935. (See also Dorothy Dehner's foreword to *John Graham's System and Dialectics of Art,* annotated from unpublished writings with a critical introduction by Marcia Epstein Allentuck, The Johns Hopkins Press, 1971.
13. John D. Graham, *System and Dialectics of Art,* Delphic Studios, New York, 1937, p. 13.
14. Graham, p. 29.
15. Graham, p. 15.
16. Sir J.G. Frazier's monumental work, *The Golden Bough,* the definitive study of comparative myths and religions, was published in the United States in 1936.
17. For a complete chronology of exhibitions and a list of exhibition places in New York in the 1920s, see *Art of the Twenties,* edited by William S. Lieberman, Museum of Modern Art, New York, 1979, "Chronology," compiled by Eila Kokkinen, pp. 10-27.
18. Dehner, in conversation, spring 1978. Exhibitions of special significance included: *Cubism and Abstract Art,* Museum of Modern Art, 1936; *Fantastic Art, Dada, Surrealism,* Museum of Modern Art, December 9, 1936 - January 17, 1937; *Picasso,*

40 Years of his Art, Museum of Modern Art, November 1939-January 1940; *Joan Miro,* Museum of Modern Art, 1941; eight Miro exhibitions were held at Pierre Matisse Gallery between 1933 and 1945; *Pablo Gargallo,* Brummer Gallery, February 21 - April 15, 1934.

19. Dehner, in conversation, spring 1978.
20. David Smith, letter to Jean Xceron, February 7, 1956, McCoy, p. 206.
21. David Smith, from notes on the 1930s, from a note/sketch-book kept about 1952, McCoy, p. 86.
22. Smith, autobiography, Gray, p. 26.
23. Adolph Gottlieb, in a response to an article by art critic Edward Alden Jewell, reviewing the 1943 exhibition of the Federation of Modern Painters and Sculptors. Gottlieb's statement, *The New York Times,* June 13, 1943.
24. Adolph Gottlieb, statement in "Jackson Pollock: An Artists' Symposium," Part I, *Art News,* April 1967, p. 31.
25. Smith, notes on the 1930s, McCoy, p. 85.
    Like many of his artist friends, Smith was assigned to various New Deal art projects. In 1934, he was a technical supervisor of mural painting for the Section of Fine Arts of the U.S. Government Treasury Relief Project, and in 1937, he was reassigned to make sculpture for the Federal Art Project of the W.P.A. In the Sylvester interview, Smith recalled that the group association with the W.P.A. was "very nice, because for the first time, collectively we belonged somewhere . . . It gave us unity, it gave us friendship, and it gave us a collective defensiveness." (McCoy, p. 168.)
26. Allentuck, *John Graham's "System and Dialectics of Art,"* p. 154. Graham listed "Matulka, Avery, Stuart Davis, Max Weber, David Smith, W. Kooning, Edgar Levy," saying "Some are just as good and some are better than the leading artists of the same generation in Europe." This appeared in the first, 1937, edition. Graham later deleted the section.
27. Dehner, in conversation, spring 1978. Also Smith, autobiography, Gray, p. 24. Smith dates the trip incorrectly as "fall of 1932."
28. Dehner, in conversation, spring 1978. Also, note 7, Gray, p. 174. Rosalind Krauss lists this work as number 15 in her catalogue raisonné, *The Sculpture of David Smith,* Garland Publishers, New York and London, 1971. If Dehner's sequence is correct, Krauss' should be revised.
29. According to Dorothy Dehner, Smith saw illustrations of Picasso and Gonzalez's welded sculpture in issues of *Cahiers d'art* about 1932. The connection between Smith's works of 1933 and Gonzalez's work is clear, in spite of the fact that some of the more complete publications of Gonzalez's sculpture came later, for example "Julio Gonzalez," *Cahiers d'art,* Vol. 10. Nos. 1-4, 1935, pp. 32-34. Individual works were illustrated earlier.
30. Dehner, in conversation, spring 1978. Terminal Iron Works, 1 Atlantic Avenue, Brooklyn, made fire escapes for schools. Smith frequently said he had learned a great deal from the men who worked there, Blackburn, Buckhorn, and a machinist called Robert Henry. (See also Smith, autobiography, Gray, p. 25.) Smith's sculpture, Blackburn, *Song of an Irish Blacksmith,* 1949-50, "was made afterwards in homage. One called Buckhorn I will do yet." (AAA ND Smith 3/258) Smith called his Bolton Landing property "Terminal Iron Works," as well.

31. AAA ND Smith E1/22, 23

32. Dehner, in conversation, spring 1978. Also, in her foreword to Allentuck: "When we were [in Paris] together, he wanted to introduce us to Picasso, but David felt he had nothing to say to him because he could not speak French. Also Graham had told him to address Picasso as *Maitre* and David was not about to call another artist *Master.*" p. xix.

33. Dehner, in conversation, spring 1978.

34. AAA ND Smith 3/453-459, 3/461,462, 3/570,571

35. Dehner, in conversation, spring 1978.

36. AAA ND Smith 3/603, 643, 644

37. AAA ND Smith 3/537, 541-543

38. AAA ND Smith 3/648

39. AAA ND Smith 4/16

40. AAA ND Smith 4/16

41. AAA ND Smith 3/501-508, 525, 528

42. AAA ND Smith 3/453

43. AAA ND Smith 3/452

44. *Cubism and Abstract Art,* at the Museum of Modern Art, 1936 included works by Archipenko, Boccioni, Brancusi, Calder, Gabo, Laurens, Lipchitz, Pevsner and Tatlin reconstructions, as well as the Gonzalez head (no. 93). Paintings by Miro and Picasso were exhibited, including the "monuments by the sea," which seem to have influenced Smith.

    Smith had little opportunity to see Picasso's sculpture first hand. The exhibition, *Picasso, 40 Years of His Art,* at the Museum of Modern Art, November 1939 - January 1940, had very little sculpture because of the difficulties of wartime transportation. *Construction,* 1928, (Monument to Apollinaire) *was* shown; its thrusting linear elements are perhaps reflected in Smith's *Portrait of the Eagle's Keeper.* Picasso's painting, *Figures on the Seashore,* 1928, was reproduced in *Cahiers d'art,* Vol. 7, Nos. 3-5, 1932, in a special section devoted to Picasso, pp. 85-196. It was exhibited in *Fantastic Art, Dada, Surrealism,* at the Museum of Modern Art in 1935, loaned by a New York collector. The exhibition also included Picasso's 1931 "dot and rod" drawings for Balzac's *Le Chef-d'oeuvre Inconnu. La Baignade,* 1923, was reproduced in the 1932 *Cahiers d'art,* and was part of the Dudensing collection, N.Y., by 1932. Reflections of all of these works can be found in Smith's sculpture and drawings of the '30s and '40s.

45. David Smith, "Sculpture; Art Form — on Architecture — New Techniques Affect Both," *Architectural Record,* October 1940, reprinted, McCoy, pp. 44-48.

46. Pablo Gargallo exhibition, Brummer Gallery, 55 East 57th Street, February 24 - April 15, 1934. *Cahiers d'art,* Vol. 2, Nos. 7-8, 1927 included an illustrated article, "Pablo Gargallo," pp. 282-286. Many of Smith's works of 1937 such as *Sculptor and Model* (Krauss 60), *Untitled* (Krauss 65 and 66) and *The Rooster* (Krauss 72), and *Leda,* 1938, as well as *Blond Head,* 1939, (Krauss 114) are closely related to Gargallo's sculptures.

47. Christian Zervos, "Quelques notes sur les sculptures de Giacometti," *Cahiers d'art,* Vol. 7, Nos. 8-10, 1932, pp. 337-342, reproduced the work, which was included in *Fantastic Art, Dada, Surrealism* at the Museum of Modern Art, 1936. The Museum owned the work by the early '30s.

48. David Smith, letter to Marian Willard, September 22, 1940.

49. Dehner, in conversation, spring 1978. Smith was declared physically unfit for service, because of sinus trouble, in 1943.

50. David Smith, letter to Robert Nathan, War Production Board, May 30, 1942, AAA ND Smith 1/280, 281. Reprinted, McCoy, p. 193.

51. Smith, letter to Robert Nathan, AAA ND Smith 1/281; McCoy, p. 193.

52. David Smith, letter to Sherman Miller, American Locomotive Works, Schenectady, New York, June 1, 1942. AAA ND Smith 1/282; reprinted McCoy, pp. 194-195. Refusal, letter from Mr. Miller, June 4, 1942, AAA ND Smith 1/28.

53. David Smith, letter to Dorothy Dehner, June 16, 1944, in Ms. Dehner's possession.

54. Smith, letter to Dehner, June 10, 1944, in Ms. Dehner's possession.

55. Dorothy Dehner, letter to Lucille Corcos, AAA ND Smith E1/1977. How different the factory stint was from sculpture making can be judged by the fact that in January 1943, Smith found it necessary to obtain a certificate from the Engineering, Science and Management War Training Program, Union College, Schenectady, declaring that he had "satisfactorily completed a course of 32 class hours in Design and Properties of Welds and Welded Structures." (Certificate dated January 21, 1943, AAA ND Smith 1/403.) The course gave Smith greater seniority at the Works, greater security as an "important" civilian member of the war effort, and eventually helped him use steel in his sculpture with greater ease and fluency.

56. This series of bronzes was conceived as a coherent whole and was always exhibited as a whole, with accompanying notes. They should be discussed as a group, and in the context of Smith's other relief sculptures. Since it was not possible to include the entire series in this exhibition, it did not seem appropriate to include two or three, in isolation.

57. David Smith, letter to J. Leroy Davidson, Assistant Director, The Walker Art Center, Minneapolis, AAA ND Smith 1/297, 298.

58. Smith, letter to Robert Nathan, AAA ND Smith 1/281, McCoy, p. 193.

59. David Smith, notes on sculpture made for Willard Gallery, AAA Willard Gallery Papers 986/804.

60. See "Selected Bibliography" for list of Greenberg writings on Smith, 1943-1964.

61. Rosalind E. Krauss, *Terminal Iron Works,* M.I.T. Press, Cambridge, Massachusetts and London, England, 1971; Chapter Two, "Smith's Imagery: The Cannon, The Totem, The Sacrifice," passim.

62. See "David Smith, Welding Master of Bolton Landing," interview with Frank O'Hara for WNDT-TV, N.Y. Excerpted, Gray, p. 124. "I don't make boy sculptures."

63. Dehner, in conversation, spring 1978.

64. AAA ND Smith 3/845

65. AAA ND Smith 3/867

66. AAA ND Smith 3/965

67. AAA ND Smith 3/611. On this notebook page, drawings of cannons used with animals and figures share space with a reference to a book on Bosch.

68. AAA ND Smith 3/612

69. For example, AAA ND Smith 3/675 and 3/838, uncatalogued pages published by Krauss, *Terminal Iron Works,* pls. 40-41, p. 57, and catalogue raisonnè figures 819, 820.

70. AAA ND Smith 4/89

71. *The Dream and Lie of Franco* was reproduced, in both states, in *Cahiers d'art,* Vol. 12, Nos. 1-3, 1937, p. 37-50. AAA ND Smith 3/765, 766, shows a group of heads, part chemical retort, part snouted monster, which seem related.

72. AAA ND Smith 4/81

73. AAA Willard Gallery Papers 986/804

74. AAA Willard Gallery Papers 986/804. The guitar-torso looks a good deal like *Perfidious Albion,* although it lacks the superimposed trident. The resemblence is heightened by the similarity between the base of *Perfidious Albion* and the mace. (Dorothy Dehner recalls Smith showing her how the sculpture could be used "as a weapon.") A similar female appears in a drawing for *Home of the Welder,* in the Fogg Museum.

75. AAA ND Smith 3/960-963

76. AAA ND Smith 3/964

77. AAA ND Smith 3/701

78. AAA ND Smith 3/842

79. AAA ND Smith 3/803

80. AAA ND Smith 3/1298 Similarly, *Maiden's Dream* seems clearly based upon a photograph of two walking stick insects on a twig. Significantly, the caption states "no males have ever been found." (AAA ND Smith 3/902) Smith captions one of the drawings "Maiden's Tears," "Combat of Walking Sticks."

81. Dehner, in conversation, spring 1978.

82. AAA ND Smith 3/886

83. Ibid.

84. AAA ND Smith 3/612. Elsewhere, Smith clipped and saved a picture story about trick photography, in which an actress "takes a trip on a giant spoon." He drew over the figure, making her into a nude. AAA ND Smith 3/913.

85. David Smith interviewed by Thomas B. Hess, June 1964. Published as "The Secret Letter," in the catalogue of the Marlborough-Gerson Gallery exhibition, October 1964. Reprinted McCoy, p. 180. A drawing for the 1950 sculpture *The Letter* (Krauss 232) AAA ND Smith 3/1283, has the superimposed phrase "the letter — you sent for me."

86. AAA ND Smith 3/695

87. David Smith, from a speech given February 15, 1940 to Local 60 of the United American Artists, in a forum on abstract art. Excerpts published in *The New York Artist,* April 1940. Reprinted, McCoy, p. 40.

88. David Smith, speech given at Williams College, December 17, 1951, reprinted McCoy, p. 78: "A pear is a violin, a pear is a woman's hips. Pear and violin have strings, woman has hair. Pear and woman have seeds, violin has notes, soft violin, hard woman, sour notes — associations can go on indefinitely . . ."

89. David Smith, letter to Franklin Page, June 23, 1949. Reprinted McCoy, pp. 203-204.

90. *Cahiers d'art* Vol. 12, Nos. 4-5, pp. 105-56, included 68 illustrations of *Guernica* and related works by Picasso.

91. AAA ND Smith 3/642

92. William Blake, frontespiece for the English translation of Burger's *Leonora,* published London, 1796; exhibited as No. 94, *Fantastic Art, Dada, Surrealism,* Museum of Modern Art, December 9, 1936 - January 17, 1937.

93. AAA ND Smith 3/663, Smith notes: "Oneiromancy in Malta they interpreted dreams provoked in the faithful that slept in cubicles still to be seen in the Hypogeum. Divination by method of *incubation.*"

94. Krauss, *Terminal Iron Works,* pp. 132-136.

95. The prevalence of biomorphic allusive forms in American art of the 1940s almost certainly is due to Miro's influence. His work was readily available, in exhibitions at the Pierre Matisse Gallery and the Museum of Modern Art, while he himself worked briefly in New York in 1946. Smith's way of linking biomorphic glyphs and spreading structures also owes something to Miro.

96. AAA ND Smith 3/843

97. Esther Gottlieb, in conversation, fall 1980.

98. Dehner, in conversation, spring, 1978. Dehner's hairstyle, in photographs of the period, makes the imagery obvious.

99. AAA ND Smith 4/75. Smith's most ambitious "linked" image preoccupied him for a long time, to judge by the numbers of notebook drawings which relate to it. The studies begin with a fairly straightforward, if stylized, rendering of a dancer and a pianist — probably made at the Boas Dancing School, where Dorothy Dehner taught. Gradually the two figures and the instrument merge. Smith eventually realized a remarkably ponderous sculpture, *Terpsichore and Euterpe,* 1947 (Krauss 214) in which the forms of dancer, pianist and piano are uniformly thickened and squared into an uncomfortable, bridge-like mass. An earlier work, 1946 (Krauss 202) explores a similar theme.

100. There's an interesting parallel, too, between an arched nude figure in one of the preparatory drawings for *Home of the Welder* (Fogg Museum) and the proffering pose of *Table Torso. Leda* shares the same swaying movement, which may be, for Smith, an attribute of femaleness. While it is obviously impossible — and suspect — to assign any specific meaning to these recurrent images, there are inevitable associations evoked by these immobilized nudes, which by extension, animate even Smith's most apparently abstract works, even those of the '50s and '60s.

101. Krauss, *Terminal Iron Works,* Chapters One and Three, passim. Also, Krauss, *David Smith, Eight Early Works,* Marlborough-Gerson Gallery, 1967, passim.

102. Krauss, *Terminal Iron Works,* p. 44.

103. David Smith, *Architectural Record,* October 1940, reprinted McCoy, pp. 44-48.

104. Smith, *Architectural Record,* McCoy, p. 45.

105. The most spectacular of these, *Helmholtzian Landscape,* 1946 (Krauss 203) reflects Smith's interest at the time of its making, in formal color theory, such as that of Helmholtz and Chabrol. The progression of brilliant hues in the piece, along with the way they bleed slightly into one another, sets up a curious, invigorating tension between surface and form.

    Perhaps the most remarkable use of polychromy in Smith's early work is to be found on the "back" of *Billard Player Construction,* where the lower part of two standing figures is suggested by complicated painting on a flat plane, while their upper portions are given by linear, pierced sculptural elements.

106. The process is sketchily documented in a series of photographs showing the development of *Cathedral,* 1950 (Krauss 229). Elements are added; little is removed or altered. In one photo, there is what appears to be a trial of a shape, in paper or cardboard, before its realization in metal. See Gray, pp. 56-57.

107. David Smith, speech at Ohio University, Athens, Ohio, April 17, 1959, reprinted McCoy, pp. 147-148.

108. AAA ND Smith 4/360, reprinted Gray, p. 17.

David Smith
The Formative Years

Figure 1
Agricola Head, 1933 *K 17*
iron and steel painted red
46.7 x 25.7 x 19.7 cm,
on base 7.9 x 25.4 x 18.4 cm
Collection of
The Estate of David Smith,
Courtesy of M. Knoedler & Co.,
New York
(Cat. no. 1)

Figure 2
Saw Head, 1933
iron painted orange, and bronze
46.4 x 30.5 x 21 cm
Collection of
The Estate of David Smith,
Courtesy of M. Knoedler & Co.,
New York
(Cat. no. 2)

29

Figure 3
Reclining Figure, 1935   *K 38*
iron
13 x 31.4 x 14 cm
Collection of
The Estate of David Smith,
Courtesy of M. Knoedler & Co.,
New York
(Cat. no. 3)

Figure 4
**Sketches for Unidentified
Structure**,
(Construction on a Fulcrum)
n.d.   *1966.38*
Pen and black ink on white paper
(page torn from a spiral pad)
14.7 x 9.9 cm
Collection of
The Fogg Art Museum,
Harvard University,
Cambridge, Massachusetts
Gift of David Smith
Exhibited only in Edmonton
(Cat. no. 57)

30

Figure 5
Construction on a Fulcrum,
1936   *K 46*
bronze and iron
35.6 x 45.7 x 7.6 cm,
on marble base
2.5 x 20.3 x 12.1 cm
Collection of
Marian Willard Johnson,
Willard Gallery, New York
(Cat. no. 4)

31

Figure 6
Billiard Player Construction,
1937   *K 53*
iron and encaustic
43.8 x 52.1 x 16.2 cm,
on wooden base
5.1 x 40.6 x 15.2 cm
Collection of
Dr. and Mrs. Arthur E. Kahn
(Cat. no. 5)

Figure 7
Notebook Drawing 3/444
David Smith Papers
On deposit,
Archives of American Art
Smithsonian Institution

Figure 8
Notebook Drawing 3/443
David Smith Papers
On deposit,
Archives of American Art
Smithsonian Institution

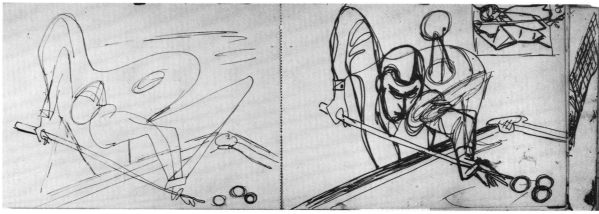

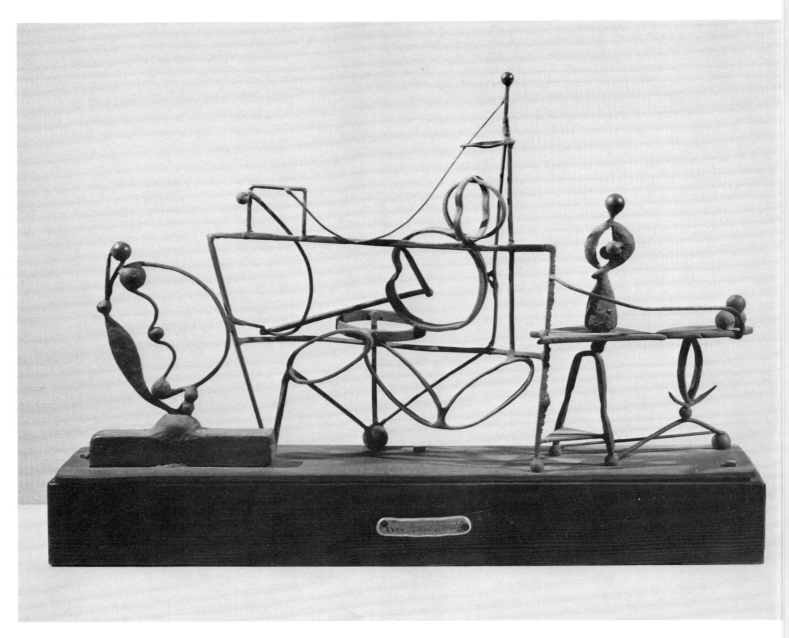

Figure 9
Interior, 1937 *K 58*
wrought and welded steel with cast
iron balls
38.7 x 66 x 13.3 cm,
on wooden base
8.6 x 67.3 x 13.3 cm
Collection of
The Weatherspoon Art Gallery,
The University of North Carolina at
Greensboro, (Anonymous Gift)
(Cat. no. 6)

Figure 10
recto:
**The Artist Photographing a Piece
of Sculpture**, 1937   *1966.34*
verso:
Three Reclining Female Nudes,
1937
recto:
pen and black ink with gray
tempera on white paper
verso:
pen and turquoise ink
17.3 x 25.4 cm
Collection of
The Fogg Art Museum,
Harvard University,
Cambridge, Massachusetts
Gift of David Smith
Exhibited only in Edmonton
(Cat. no. 43)

Figure 11
Vertical Figure (Construction Perpendicular), 1937   *K 73*
iron
61 x 17.8 x 14.9 cm, on iron base
2.5 x 17.8 x 15.2 cm
Private Collection
(Cat. no. 7)

Figure 12
Head, 1938 *K 82*
cast iron and steel
50.2 x 25.4 x 29.2 cm
Collection of The Museum of
Modern Art, New York.
Gift of Charles E. Merrill
(Cat no. 9)

Figure 13
Head, 1938   *K 81*
iron painted red
33 x 22.9 x 22.9 cm,
on wooden base
11.8 x 11.8 x 11.8 cm
Collection of Edward T. Riley
(Cat. no. 8)

Figure 13
Head, 1938 *K 81*
iron painted red
33 x 22.9 x 22.9 cm,
on wooden base
11.8 x 11.8 x 11.8 cm
Collection of Edward T. Riley
(Cat. no. 8)

Figure 14
Leda, 1938   *K 84*
steel painted brown
50.8 x 21 x 25.4 cm
Collection of
Mrs. Douglas Crockwell
(Cat. no. 10)

40

Figure 14
Leda, 1938   *K 84*
steel painted brown
50.8 x 21 x 25.4 cm
Collection of
Mrs. Douglas Crockwell
(Cat. no. 10)

41

Figure 15
Interior for Exterior, 1939   *K 122*
steel and bronze
45.7 x 55.9 x 59.7 cm, on base
3.3 x 29.9 x 28.3 cm
Collection of
Mr. and Mrs. Orin Raphael
(Cat no. 11)

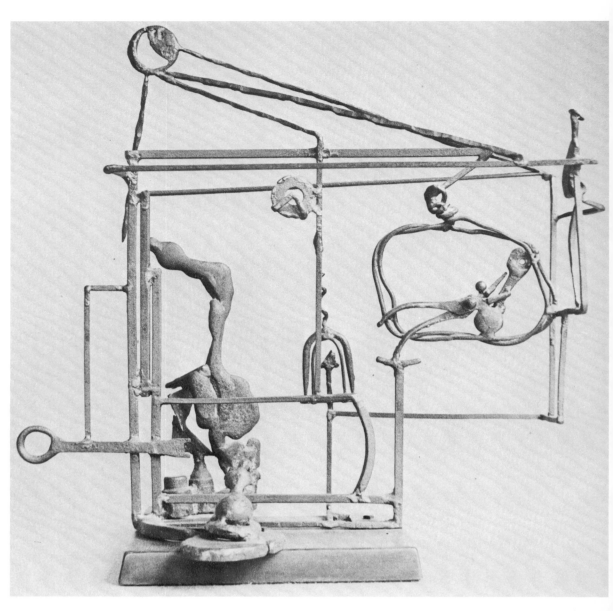

Figure 16
Giacometti, Alberto
The Palace at 4 a.m., 1932-33
construction in wood, glass, wire,
string
63.5 x 71.8 x 40 cm
Collection of
The Museum of Modern Art,
New York

42

Figure 17
Vertical Structure, 1939   *K 128*
steel with copper
116.5 x 85.1 x 73 cm on base
Collection of
The Estate of David Smith,
Courtesy of M. Knoedler & Co.,
New York
(Cat. no. 12)

43

Figure 18
Head as a Still Life, 1940   *K 137*
cast iron and bronze
39.4 x 44.5 x 19.7 cm
Collection of
The Estate of David Smith,
Courtesy of M. Knoedler & Co.,
New York
(Cat. no. 14)

Figure 19
Head as a Still Life,
c. 1939–40 *73-39.9*
pen and ink on paper
11.4 x 13.7 cm
Collection of
The Estate of David Smith,
Courtesy of M. Knoedler & Co.,
New York
(Cat. no. 48)

Figure 20
Bathers, 1940   *K 134*
steel
35.6 x 35.6 x 45.7 cm,
on wooden base
3.8 x 19.1 x 38.1 cm
Collection of
Marian Willard Johnson,
Willard Gallery, New York
(Cat. no. 13)

Figure 20
Bathers, 1940   *K 134*
steel
35.6 x 35.6 x 45.7 cm,
on wooden base
3.8 x 19.1 x 38.1 cm
Collection of
Marian Willard Johnson,
Willard Gallery, New York
(Cat. no. 13)

Figure 21
Widow's Lament, 1942 *K 150*
forged and fabricated steel
and bronze
34.3 x 50.8 x 16.8 cm,
on base 6.4 x 20.3 x 12.7 cm
Private Collection
(Cat. no. 15)

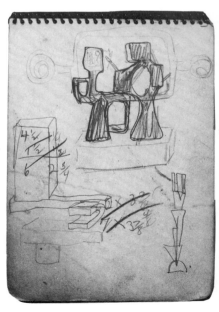

Figure 22
Notebook Drawing, 3/768
David Smith Papers
On deposit, Archives of
American Art
Smithsonian Institution

48

Figure 23
Table Torso, 1942   *K 149*
bronze
25.4 x 10.8 x 14.3 cm
Collection of Brandeis University,
The Rose Art Museum, The Charna
Stone Cowan Student Loan
Collection
(Cat. no. 16)

Figure 24
Atrocity, 1943   *K 154*
bronze
12.1 x 16.5 x 8.9 cm
Private Collection
(Cat. no. 17)

Figure 25
Ritual, 1943   *K 156*
forged steel
20.8 x 24.8 x 11.6 cm,
on wooden base
3.3 x 14.4 x 9.6 cm
Collection of The Hirshhorn
Museum and Sculpture Garden,
The Smithsonian Institution
(Cat. no. 18)

Figure 26
Medals for Dishonor,
c. 1938-39   *75-38.92*
ink and wash on paper
40 x 47.5 cm
Collection of
The Estate of David Smith,
Courtesy of M. Knoedler & Co.,
New York
(Cat. no. 46)

51

Figure 27
Sewing Machine, 1943   *K 158*
Danby Blue marble
30.5 x 55.9 x 6.4 cm,
on base 4.5 x 61 x 12.7 cm
Courtesy of
The André Emmerich Gallery
(Cat. no. 19)

Figure 28
Big Rooster, 1945 *K 168*
forged and welded steel
41.9 x 54 x 39.7 cm
Collection of The Hirshhorn
Museum and Sculpture Garden,
The Smithsonian Institution
(Cat. no. 21)

Figure 29
Big Rooster,
c. 1938-39 *75-38.54*
ink with grey pastel on paper
30.3 x 22.5 cm
Collection of
The Estate of David Smith,
Courtesy of M. Knoedler & Co.,
New York
(Cat. no. 44)

Figure 30
Big Rooster,
c. 1938-39 *75-38.68*
black ink on paper
30.2 x 22.8 cm
Collection of
The Estate of David Smith,
Courtesy of M. Knoedler & Co.,
New York
(Cat. no. 45)

53

Figure 31
Home of the Welder,
1945   *K 180*
steel
53.3 x 44.1 x 35.6 cm
Collection of
The Estate of David Smith,
Courtesy of M. Knoedler & Co.,
New York
(Cat. no. 22)

Figure 32
**Sketches for "Home of the Welder":
Wife as Locomotive Parts,**
1945   *1966.36*
India and blue inks with white
tempera and brown wash over
graphite and touches of red pencil
25.4 x 18.5 cm
Collection of
The Fogg Art Museum,
Harvard University,
Cambridge, Massachusetts
Gift of David Smith
Exhibited only in Edmonton
(Cat. no. 56)

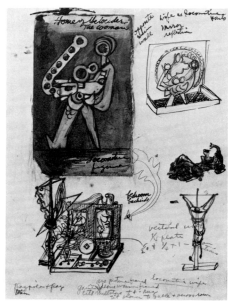

54

Figure 31
Home of the Welder,
1945   *K 180*
steel
53.3 x 44.1 x 35.6 cm
Collection of
The Estate of David Smith,
Courtesy of M. Knoedler & Co.,
New York
(Cat. no. 22)

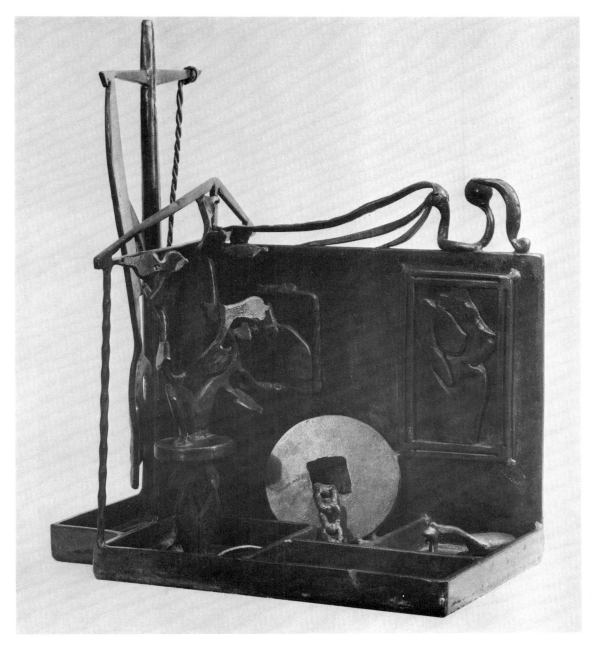

Figure 33
recto:
Sketches for "Home of the Welder",
1945   *1966.35*
verso:
Unidentified Design, 1945
recto:
pen and wash with India and blue
inks over graphite
on white paper
verso:
graphite
25.4 x 18.5 cm
Collection of
The Fogg Art Museum,
Harvard University,
Cambridge, Massachusetts
Gift of David Smith
Exhibited only in Edmonton
(Cat. no. 55)

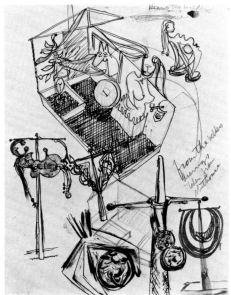

55

Figure 34
Pillar of Sunday, 1945   *K 184*
painted steel
78.7 x 42.2 x 21.6 cm,
on base 4.8 x 15.9 x 15.2 cm
Collection of The Indiana
University Art Museum
Exhibited only in Edmonton
(Cat. no. 26)

Figure 35
recto:
Sketches for "Pillar of Sunday",
1945   *1966.41*
verso:
Box Construction, 1945
recto:
graphite, pen with blue and black
inks and black tempera
verso:
graphite
25.4 x 18.4 cm
Collection of
The Fogg Art Museum,
Harvard University,
Cambridge, Massachusetts
Gift of David Smith
Exhibited only in Edmonton
(Cat. no. 60)

Figure 36
Perfidious Albion, 1945   *K 183*
bronze and cast iron
36.5 x 11.4 x 6.7 cm
Collection of
The Estate of David Smith,
Courtesy of M. Knoedler & Co.,
New York
(Cat. no. 24)

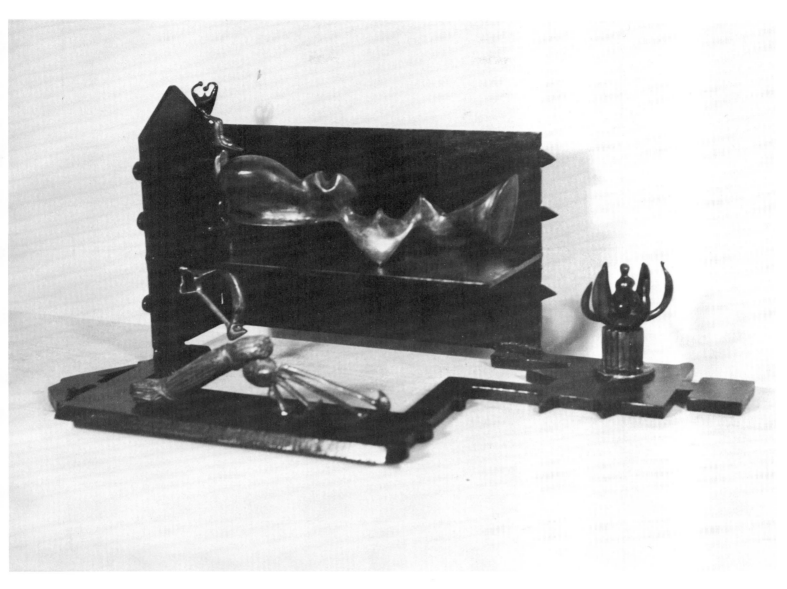

Figure 37
Reliquary House, 1945   *K 186*
bronze and steel painted black
31.8 x 63.5 x 29.9 cm
Collection of
Mr. and Mrs. David Mirvish
(Cat. no. 27)

Figure 38
Untitled (Woman with Guitar and
Bird), 1946   *73-46.5*
tempera on paper
58.1 x 74 cm
Collection of
The Estate of David Smith,
Courtesy of M. Knoedler & Co.,
New York
(Cat. no. 62)

59

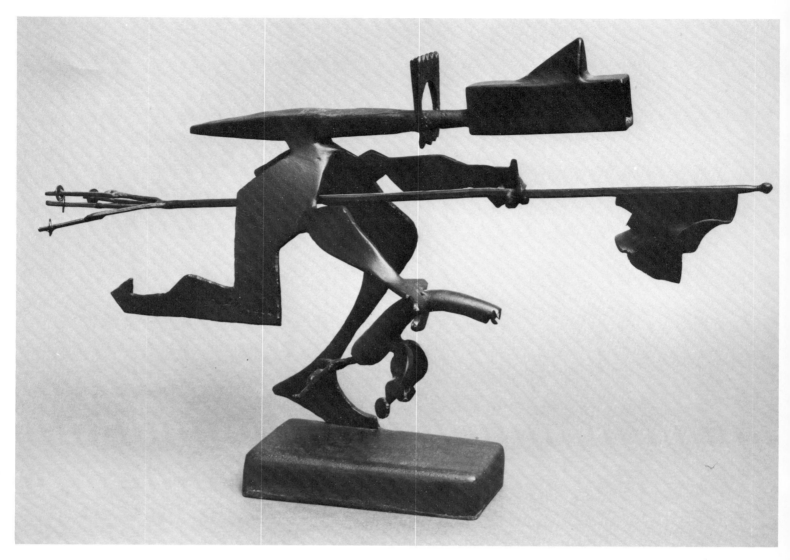

Figure 39
War Spectre, 1944   *K 162*
steel painted black
29.2 x 15.2 x 55.9 cm,
on base 6.4 x 20.3 x 10.2 cm
Collection of The Museum of Fine
Arts, Houston
Exhibited only in
Edmonton and Seattle
(Cat. no. 20)

Figure 40
recto:
False Peace Spectre,
1945   *1966.40*
verso:
Sketches for the Spectre, 1945
recto: graphite and blue ink with
black and purple tempera
verso:
graphite
25.4 x 18.6 cm
Collection of
The Fogg Art Museum,
Harvard University,
Cambridge, Massachusetts
Gift of David Smith
Exhibited only in Edmonton
(Cat. no. 59)

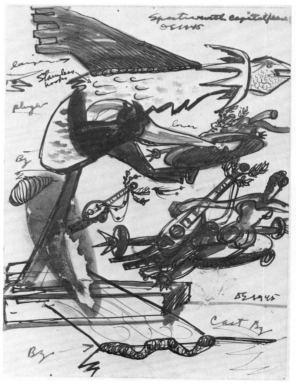

Figure 41
Spectre Riding the Golden Ass,
1945   *K 189*
bronze
29.9 x 31.8 x 10.2 cm
Collection of The Detroit Institute
of Fine Arts,
Gift of Robert H. Tannahill
(Cat. no. 28)

Figure 42
Steel Drawing I, 1945   *K 190*
steel
56.5 x 66 x 15.2 cm
Collection of The Hirshhorn
Museum and Sculpture Garden,
The Smithsonian Institution
(Cat. no. 29)

Figure 43
Landscape with Strata,
1946   *K 204*
steel, bronze and stainless steel
42.9 x 53.3 x 21 cm,
on base 6.4 x 27.9 x 11.4 cm
Collection of
Dr. and Mrs. Arthur E. Kahn
(Cat. no. 30)

Figure 44
Spectre of Mother, 1946   *K 210*
steel and stainless steel
51.8 x 50 x 23.5 cm,
on base 7.6 x 33 x 15.2 cm
Collection of
Mr. and Mrs. Sidney M. Feldman
(Cat. no. 31)

64

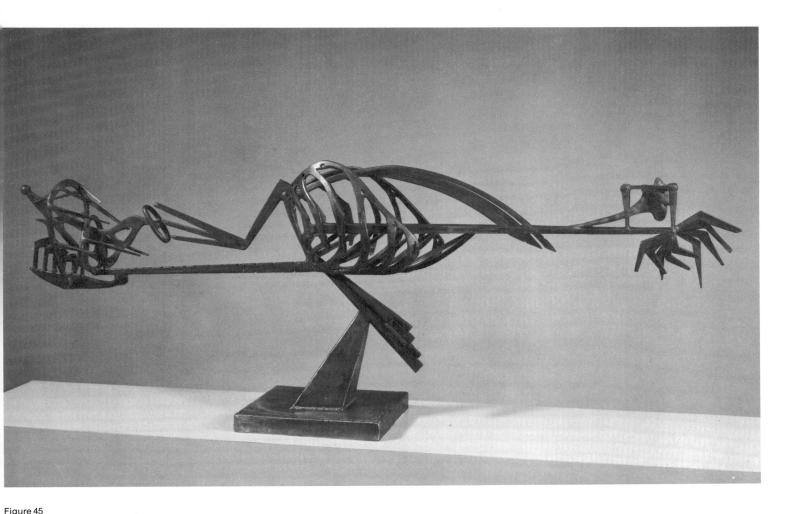

Figure 45
Royal Bird, 1948 *K 219*
steel, bronze and stainless steel
58.4 x 152.4 x 20.3 cm
Collection of
The Walker Art Centre,
Minneapolis
Gift of
The T.B. Walker Foundation
Exhibited only in Edmonton
(Cat. no. 33)

66

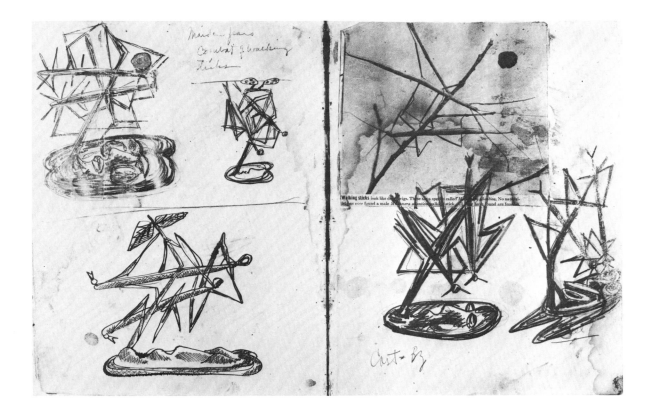

Figure 47
Notebook Drawing 3/902
Smith Papers,
On deposit, Archives of
American Art
Smithsonian Institution

Figure 48
Notebook Drawing 4/83
(left side)
Smith Papers,
On deposit, Archives of
American Art
Smithsonian Institution

Figure 49
Portrait of the Eagle's Keeper,
1948–49   *K 227*
steel and bronze
96.5 x 32.7 x 57.8 cm,
on circular base
3.8 x 27.3 cm diameter
Collection of
Helen Frankenthaler
Exhibited only in Edmonton
(Cat. no. 34)

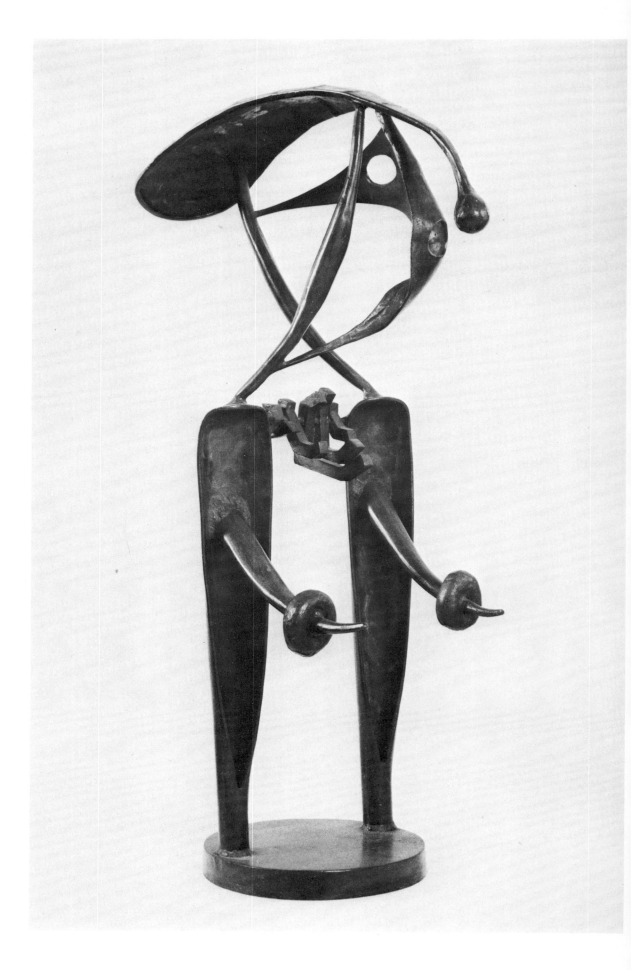

68

Figure 49
Portrait of the Eagle's Keeper,
1948-49   *K 227*
steel and bronze
96.5 x 32.7 x 57.8 cm,
on circular base
3.8 x 27.3 cm diameter
Collection of
Helen Frankenthaler
Exhibited only in Edmonton
(Cat. no. 34)

Figure 50
Royal Incubator, 1949   *K 234*
steel, bronze and silver
94 x 97.5 x 25.1 cm
Collection of
Mr. and Mrs. Bagley Wright
Exhibited only in
Edmonton and Seattle
(Cat. no. 35)

Figure 51
Notebook Drawing 4/83
(right side)
Smith Papers
On deposit, Archives of
American Art
Smithsonian Institution

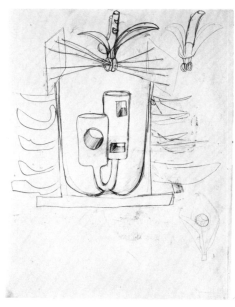

70

Figure 52
Royal Incubator,
c. 1949   *73-50.2*
black egg ink on paper
51.1 x 66.3 cm
Collection of
The Estate of David Smith,
Courtesy of M. Knoedler & Co.,
New York
(Cat. no. 66)

Figure 53
Notebook Drawing 4/85
Smith Papers
On deposit, Archives of
American Art
Smithsonian Institution

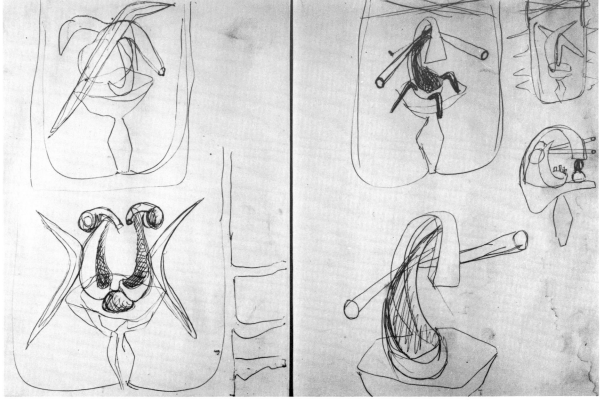

71

Figure 54
Blackburn, Song of an Irish Blacksmith, 1949-50   *K 228*
steel and bronze
117.5 x 103.5 x 61 cm,
on base 20.3 x 18.4 cm diameter
Collection of The Wilhelm
Lehmbruck Museum,
Duisberg, Germany
Exhibited only in
Edmonton and Seattle
(Cat. no. 36)

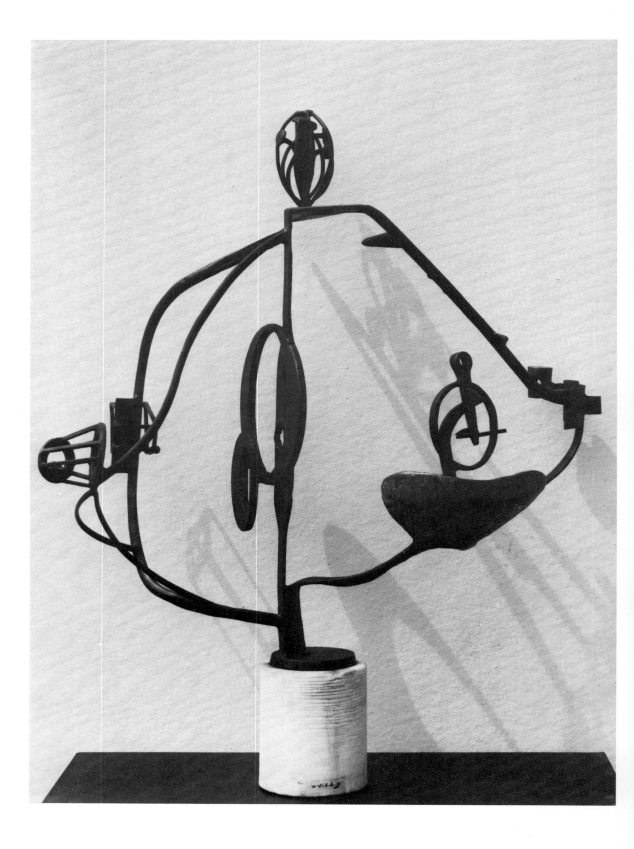

List of Works
Sculpture

(Height precedes width precedes depth. The letter "K" followed by a number stands for the inventory number in the catalogue raisonné, The Sculpture of David Smith, *prepared by Rosalind Krauss.)*

1. **Agricola Head**, 1933   *K 17*
   iron and steel painted red
   46.7 x 25.7 x 19.7 cm, on base 7.9 x 25.4 x 18.4 cm
   Collection of The Estate of David Smith,
   Courtesy of M. Knoedler & Co., New York

2. **Saw Head**, 1933
   iron painted orange, and bronze
   46.4 x 30.5 x 21 cm
   Collection of The Estate of David Smith,
   Courtesy of M. Knoedler & Co., New York

3. **Reclining Figure**, 1935   *K 38*
   iron
   13 x 31.4 x 14 cm
   Collection of The Estate of David Smith,
   Courtesy of M. Knoedler & Co., New York

4. **Construction on a Fulcrum**, 1936   *K 46*
   bronze and iron
   35.6 x 45.7 x 7.6 cm, on marble base
   2.5 x 20.3 x 12.1 cm
   Collection of Marian Willard Johnson,
   Willard Gallery, New York

5. **Billiard Player Construction**, 1937   *K 53*
   iron and encaustic
   43.8 x 52.1 x 16.2 cm, on wooden base
   5.1 x 40.6 x 15.2 cm
   Collection of Dr. and Mrs. Arthur E. Kahn

6. **Interior**, 1937   *K 58*
   wrought and welded steel with cast iron balls
   38.7 x 66 x 13.3 cm, on wooden base
   8.6 x 67.3 x 13.3 cm
   Collection of The Weatherspoon Art Gallery,
   The University of North Carolina at Greensboro,
   (Anonymous Gift)

7. **Vertical Figure (Construction Perpendicular)**,
   1937   *K 73*
   iron
   61 x 17.8 x 14.9 cm, on iron base
   2.5 x 17.8 x 15.2 cm
   Private Collection

8. **Head**, 1938   *K 81*
   iron painted red
   33 x 22.9 x 22.9 cm, on wooden base
   11.8 x 11.8 x 11.8 cm
   Collection of Edward T. Riley

9. **Head**, 1938   *K 82*
   cast iron and steel
   50.2 x 25.4 x 29.2 cm
   Collection of The Museum of Modern Art,
   New York. Gift of Charles E. Merrill

10. **Leda**, 1938   *K 84*
    steel painted brown
    50.8 x 21 x 25.4 cm
    Collection of Mrs. Douglas Crockwell

11. **Interior for Exterior**, 1939   *K 122*
    steel and bronze
    45.7 x 55.9 x 59.7 cm, on base 3.3 x 29.9 x 28.3 cm
    Collection of Mr. and Mrs. Orin Raphael

12. **Vertical Structure**, 1939   *K 128*
    steel with copper
    116.5 x 85.1 x 73 cm on base
    Collection of The Estate of David Smith,
    Courtesy of M. Knoedler & Co., New York

13. **Bathers**, 1940   *K 134*
    steel
    35.6 x 35.6 x 45.7 cm, on wooden base
    3.8 x 19.1 x 38.1 cm
    Collection of Marian Willard Johnson,
    Willard Gallery, New York

14. **Head as a Still Life**, 1940   *K 137*
    cast iron and bronze
    39.4 x 44.5 x 19.7 cm
    Collection of The Estate of David Smith,
    Courtesy of M. Knoedler & Co., New York

15. **Widow's Lament**, 1942   *K 150*
    forged and fabricated steel and bronze
    34.3 x 50.8 x 16.8 cm, on base 6.4 x 20.3 x 12.7 cm
    Private Collection

16. **Table Torso**, 1942   *K 149*
    bronze
    25.4 x 10.8 x 14.3 cm
    Collection of Brandeis University, The Rose Art
    Museum, The Charna Stone Cowan Student Loan
    Collection

17. **Atrocity**, 1943   *K 154*
    bronze
    12.1 x 16.5 x 8.9 cm
    Private Collection

18. **Ritual**, 1943   *K 156*
    forged steel
    20.8 x 24.8 x 11.6 cm, on wooden base
    3.3 x 14.4 x 9.6 cm
    Collection of The Hirshhorn Museum and
    Sculpture Garden,
    The Smithsonian Institution

19. **Sewing Machine**, 1943   *K 158*
    Danby Blue marble
    30.5 x 55.9 x 6.4 cm, on base 4.5 x 61 x 12.7 cm
    Courtesy of The André Emmerich Gallery

20. **War Spectre**, 1944   *K 162*
    steel painted black
    29.2 x 15.2 x 55.9 cm, on base 6.4 x 20.3 x 10.2 cm
    Collection of The Museum of Fine Arts, Houston
    Exhibited only in Edmonton and Seattle

21. **Big Rooster**, 1945   *K 168*
    forged and welded steel
    41.9 x 54 x 39.7 cm
    Collection of The Hirshhorn Museum and
    Sculpture Garden,
    The Smithsonian Institution

22. **Home of the Welder**, 1945   *K 180*
    steel
    53.3 x 44.1 x 35.6 cm
    Collection of The Estate of David Smith,
    Courtesy of M. Knoedler & Co., New York

23. **Perfidious Albion**, 1945   *K 183*
    bronze and cast iron
    36.5 x 11.4 x 6.7 cm
    Collection of Dorothy Dehner

24. **Perfidious Albion**, 1945   *K 183*
bronze and cast iron
36.5 x 11.4 x 6.7 cm
Collection of The Estate of David Smith,
Courtesy of M. Knoedler & Co., New York

25. **Perfidious Albion**, 1945   *K 183*
bronze and cast iron
36.5 x 11.4 x 6.7 cm
Collection of Mrs. Douglas Crockwell

26. **Pillar of Sunday**, 1945   *K 184*
painted steel
78.7 x 42.2 x 21.6 cm, on base 4.8 x 15.9 x 15.2 cm
Collection of The Indiana University Art Museum
Exhibited only in Edmonton

27. **Reliquary House**, 1945   *K 186*
bronze and steel painted black
31.8 x 63.5 x 29.9 cm
Collection of Mr. and Mrs. David Mirvish

28. **Spectre Riding the Golden Ass**, 1945   *K 189*
bronze
29.9 x 31.8 x 10.2 cm
Collection of The Detroit Institute of Fine Arts,
Gift of Robert H. Tannahill

29. **Steel Drawing I**, 1945   *K 190*
steel
56.5 x 66 x 15.2 cm
Collection of The Hirshhorn Museum and
Sculpture Garden,
The Smithsonian Institution

30. **Landscape with Strata**, 1946   *K 204*
steel, bronze and stainless steel
42.9 x 53.3 x 21 cm, on base 6.4 x 27.9 x 11.4 cm
Collection of Dr. and Mrs. Arthur E. Kahn

31. **Spectre of Mother**, 1946   *K 210*
steel and stainless steel
51.8 x 50 x 23.5 cm, on base 7.6 x 33 x 15.2 cm
Collection of Mr. and Mrs. Sidney M. Feldman

32. **Maiden's Dream**, 1947-48   *K 224*
bronze
68.6 x 49.5 x 50.8 cm
Collection of The Estate of David Smith,
Courtesy of M. Knoedler & Co., New York

33. **Royal Bird**, 1948   *K 219*
steel, bronze and stainless steel
58.4 x 152.4 x 20.3 cm
Collection of The Walker Art Centre, Minneapolis
Gift of The T.B. Walker Foundation
Exhibited only in Edmonton

34. **Portrait of the Eagle's Keeper**, 1948-49   *K 227*
steel and bronze
96.5 x 32.7 x 57.8 cm,
on circular base 3.8 x 27.3 cm diameter
Collection of Helen Frankenthaler
Exhibited only in Edmonton

35. **Royal Incubator**, 1949   *K 234*
steel, bronze and silver
94 x 97.5 x 25.1 cm
Collection of Mr. and Mrs. Bagley Wright
Exhibited only in Edmonton and Seattle

36. **Blackburn, Song of an Irish Blacksmith**, 1949-50
K 228
steel and bronze
117.5 x 103.5 x 61 cm,
on base 20.3 x 18.4 cm diameter
Collection of The Wilhelm Lehmbruck Museum,
Duisberg, Germany
Exhibited only in Edmonton and Seattle

Drawings

37. **Untitled (Island Theme)**, 1932 *73-32.3*
pen and ink with green and blue wash on paper
27.9 x 21.5 cm
Collection of The Estate of David Smith,
Courtesy of M. Knoedler & Co., New York

38. **Untitled**, 1933 *73-33.1*
No. 22 (One of 27 drawings)
black ink on paper
35 x 41.8 cm
Collection of The Estate of David Smith,
Courtesy of M. Knoedler & Co., New York

39. **Study for Billiard Player**, c. 1935 *73-35.1*
pencil and black ink on handmade rice paper
43.6 x 56.9 cm
Collection of The Estate of David Smith,
Courtesy of M. Knoedler & Co., New York

40. **Untitled** (sculptural - reclining figure), 1937
73-37.3
pastel on paper mounted on cardboard
44.5 x 57.9 cm
Collection of The Estate of David Smith,
Courtesy of M. Knoedler & Co., New York

41. **Untitled** (sculptural - linear and form), c. 1936-37
73-37.5
black with wash on paper
43.3 x 55.6 cm
Collection of The Estate of David Smith,
Courtesy of M. Knoedler & Co., New York

42. **Photographer Leo Lances Taking Picture of
Reclining Figure**, 1937 *73-37.13*
ink and wash on paper
24.4 x 18.3 cm
Collection of The Estate of David Smith,
Courtesy of M. Knoedler & Co., New York

43. recto:
The Artist Photographing a Piece of Sculpture,
1937 *1966.34*
verso:
Three Reclining Female Nudes, 1937
recto:
pen and black ink with gray tempera on white
paper
verso:
pen and turquoise ink
17.3 x 25.4 cm
Collection of The Fogg Art Museum, Harvard
University,
Cambridge, Massachusetts
Gift of David Smith
Exhibited only in Edmonton

44. **Big Rooster**, c. 1938-39 *75-38.54*
ink with grey pastel on paper
30.3 x 22.5 cm
Collection of The Estate of David Smith,
Courtesy of M. Knoedler & Co., New York

45. **Big Rooster**, c. 1938-39 *75-38.68*
black ink on paper
30.2 x 22.8 cm
Collection of The Estate of David Smith,
Courtesy of M. Knoedler & Co., New York

46. **Medals for Dishonor**, c. 1938-39 *75-38.92*
ink and wash on paper
40 x 47.5 cm
Collection of The Estate of David Smith,
Courtesy of M. Knoedler & Co., New York

47. **Sculpt 1938** (broken - restored - repainted), 1938
73-39.1
oil pastel on Glasgow paper
56 x 43 cm
Collection of The Estate of David Smith,
Courtesy of M. Knoedler & Co., New York

48. **Head as a Still Life**, c. 1939-40 *73-39.9*
pen and ink on paper
11.4 x 13.7 cm
Collection of The Estate of David Smith,
Courtesy of M. Knoedler & Co., New York

49. **Nude**, 1940 *73-40.2*
No. 5 (one in a series of 12)
ink and tempera on Glasgow paper
55.9 x 43 cm
Collection of The Estate of David Smith,
Courtesy of M. Knoedler & Co., New York

50. **Hope Chest** (sculptural), 1941 *73-41.1 A*
pen and ink with grey pastel on paper
22 x 29 cm
Collection of The Estate of David Smith,
Courtesy of M. Knoedler & Co., New York

51. **Hopechest**, 1941 *73-41.1 B*
pen and ink with grey pastel on paper
22 x 29.3 cm
Collection of The Estate of David Smith,
Courtesy of M. Knoedler & Co., New York

52. **Cockfight Variation 2**, c. 1944 *73-44.4*
ink with wash and pastel on aquarelle paper
50 x 63.6 cm
Collection of The Estate of David Smith,
Courtesy of M. Knoedler & Co., New York

53. **Steel Drawing**, c. 1945 *73-50.35 A*
pen and ink on paper
25.3 x 18.1 cm
Collection of The Estate of David Smith,
Courtesy of M. Knoedler & Co., New York

54. **Steel Drawing**, c. 1945 *73-50.35 B*
pen and ink on paper
25.3 x 18.1 cm
Collection of The Estate of David Smith,
Courtesy of M. Knoedler & Co., New York

55. recto:
Sketches for "Home of the Welder", 1945 *1966.35*
verso:
Unidentified Design, 1945
recto:
pen and wash with India and blue inks over
graphite on white paper
verso:
graphite
25.4 x 18.5 cm
Collection of The Fogg Art Museum, Harvard
University,
Cambridge, Massachusetts
Gift of David Smith
Exhibited only in Edmonton

56. **Sketches for "Home of the Welder": Wife as Loco-motive Parts**, 1945   *1966.36*
India and blue inks with white tempera and brown wash over graphite and touches of red pencil
25.4 x 18.5 cm
Collection of The Fogg Art Museum, Harvard University,
Cambridge, Massachusetts
Gift of David Smith
Exhibited only in Edmonton

57. **Sketches for Unidentified Structure,**
(Construction on a Fulcrum) n.d.   *1966.38*
Pen and black ink on white paper (page torn from a spiral pad)
14.7 x 9.9 cm
Collection of The Fogg Art Museum, Harvard University,
Cambridge, Massachusetts
Gift of David Smith
Exhibited only in Edmonton

58. recto:
Two Unidentified Structures, n.d. *1966.39*
verso:
Arabesque, n.d.
recto:
graphite, pen with India ink and an area of black spatter
verso:
graphite (page torn from a spiral pad)
15 x 9.9 cm
Collection of The Fogg Art Museum, Harvard University,
Cambridge, Massachusetts
Gift of David Smith
Exhibited only in Edmonton

59. recto:
False Peace Spectre, 1945   *1966.40*
verso:
Sketches for the Spectre, 1945
recto: graphite and blue ink with black and purple tempera
verso:
graphite
25.4 x 18.6 cm
Collection of The Fogg Art Museum, Harvard University,
Cambridge, Massachusetts
Gift of David Smith
Exhibited only in Edmonton

60. recto:
Sketches for "Pillar of Sunday", 1945   *1966.41*
verso:
Box Construction, 1945
recto:
graphite, pen with blue and black inks and black tempera
verso:
graphite
25.4 x 18.4 cm
Collection of The Fogg Art Museum, Harvard University,
Cambridge, Massachusetts
Gift of David Smith
Exhibited only in Edmonton

61. **Pillar of Sunday**, 1945   *73-45.1*
ink with wash on paper
25.6 x 18.2 cm
Collection of The Estate of David Smith,
Courtesy of M. Knoedler & Co., New York

62. **Untitled** (Woman with Guitar and Bird), 1946
73-46.5
tempera on paper
58.1 x 74 cm
Collection of The Estate of David Smith,
Courtesy of M. Knoedler & Co., New York

63. **Untitled**, 1946   *73-46.12*
egg ink with tempera and oil on paper
50.7 x 65.7 cm
Collection of The Estate of David Smith,
Courtesy of M. Knoedler & Co., New York

64. **Untitled** (Nude), 1949   *73-49.1*
pen and ink with pink wash on paper
58 x 81 cm
Collection of The Estate of David Smith,
Courtesy of M. Knoedler & Co., New York

65. **Untitled** (abstract painting with figures), 1949
73-49.7
tempera and black egg ink on paper
43.5 x 58 cm
Collection of The Estate of David Smith,
Courtesy of M. Knoedler & Co., New York

66. **Royal Incubator**, c. 1949   *73-50.2*
black egg ink on paper
51.1 x 66.3 cm
Collection of The Estate of David Smith,
Courtesy of M. Knoedler & Co., New York

67. **Untitled**, 1950   *73-50.32*
black ink and tempera wash on paper
45.7 x 58 cm
Collection of The Estate of David Smith,
Courtesy of M. Knoedler & Co., New York

Biography

1906	Born March 8, Decatur, Indiana
1921	Family moves to Paulding, Ohio
1924	Ohio University, Athens, Ohio
1925	Notre Dame University (two weeks)
1926	Moves to Washington, D.C. Attends George Washington University (one semester)
	Moves to New York
1927	Marries Dorothy Dehner, December 24
1927-1932	Full-time student at the Art Students League
1928	Moves to Brooklyn Heights
1928-1929	Private painting classes with Jan Matulka
1929	Buys farm in Bolton Landing, N.Y.
1930	Meets John Graham
1931-1932	(October to June) Visits Virgin Islands. First sculpture
1933	First welded steel sculpture
1935	To Europe (October) Winter in Greece Visits Paris, London, U.S.S.R.
1936	Returns to U.S., July 4
1938	First one-man exhibition, sculpture and drawings, Willard Gallery, January
1939	Shows with American Abstract Artists, Riverside Museum
1940	One-man exhibition, Neumann-Willard Gallery, March Moves to Bolton Landing *Medals for Dishonor* shown at Willard Gallery
1941	One Man Exhibitions: Kalamazoo Institute of Art, Kalamazoo, Michigan; St. Paul Gallery and School of Art, St. Paul, Minnesota; Minnesota University Gallery, Minneapolis
1942	Shows with Artists for Victory, Metropolitan Museum of Art One Man exhibition, Walker Art Center, Minneapolis
1942-44	Works at American Locomotive Company, Schenectady, N.Y.
1943	One-man exhibitions: Willard Gallery; Skidmore College, Saratoga Springs, N.Y. Shows with Dorothy Dehner, Albany Institute and School of Art, Albany, N.Y.
1944	Meets Clement Greenberg
1946	Retrospective exhibition of works from 1936-45 (54 works) at Willard and Bucholz Galleries
1947	Retrospective exhibition circulated in U.S. by American Association of University Women
1948	One man exhibition, University of Louisville, Louisville, Kentucky Shows in *Abstract-Surrealist* exhibition, Art Institute of Chicago
1948-1950	Teaches at Sara Lawrence College, Bronxville, N.Y.
1950	Guggenheim Fellowship One man exhibition, Willard Gallery
1951	Guggenheim Fellowship (renewed) One man exhibitions: Bennington College, Bennington, Vermont; Willard Gallery U.S. representation at Sao Paulo First Biennal, Sao Paulo, Brazil Shown in *American Sculpture*, Metropolitan Museum of Art, N.Y.
1952	One man exhibitions: Willard-Kleeman Galleries; Walker Art Center, Minneapolis; Williams College Museum of Art, Williamstown, Massachusetts Divorced from Dorothy Dehner
1953	Teaches at University of Arkansas, Fayetteville, Arkansas One man exhibitions: Kootz Gallery, N.Y.; University of Arkansas, Fayetteville; Catholic University, Washington, D.C. Marries Jean Freas
1954	One man exhibitions: Willard Gallery; Cincinnati Art Museum, Cincinnati, Ohio Daughter, Rebecca born
1955	Daughter Candida born
1956	One man exhibition, Willard Gallery Shows in *International Exhibition of Contemporary Sculpture*, Musee Rodin, Paris
1957	Retrospective Exhibition, Museum of Modern Art

1958	U.S. representative at XXIX Biennale, Venice Shows in U.S. Pavillion, World's Fair, Brussels
1959	One man exhibition, paintings and drawings, French & Co., N.Y. U.S. representation, V Sao Paulo Bienal, Sao Paulo, Brazil Shows in *Dokumenta II: Skulptur,* Kassel, Germany
1960	One man exhibitions: French & Co., N.Y.; Everett Ellin Gallery, Los Angeles Special issue of *ARTS* magazine devoted to Smith
1961	One man exhibitions: Carnegie Institute, Pittsburgh; Otto Gerson Gallery, N.Y. (circulated by Museum of Modern Art in U.S.) Divorced from Jean Freas
1962	Invited to spend a month in Italy making sculpture for the Fourth Festival of Two Worlds, Spoleto, Italy. Works in Voltri, exhibition in Spoleto
1963	One man exhibitions: drawings, Balin-Traube Gallery, N.Y.; drawings, circulated by Museum of Modern Art in the U.S. and Canada
1964	One man exhibitions: Institute of Contemporary Art, University of Pennsylvania, Philadelphia; Marlborough-Gerson Gallery, N.Y. Shows at *Documenta III,* Kassel, Germany
1965	Appointed to National Council on the Arts by President Lyndon B. Johnson Dies following automobile crash near Bennington, Vermont, May 23rd.

Selected Bibliography

Allentuck, Marcia Epstein, *John Graham's "System and Dialectics of Art,"* annotated from unpublished writings, The Johns Hopkins Press, 1971

Carmean, E.A., Jr. and Rathstone, Eliza E., with Hess, Thomas B., *American Art at Mid-Century, Subjects of the Artist,* (ex. cat.) National Gallery of Art, Washington, D.C., 1978

Cone, Jane Harrison, *David Smith 1906-1965: A Retrospective Exhibition,* (exh. cat.) Fogg Art Museum, Harvard University, Cambridge, Mass., 1966

Cummings, Paul, *David Smith, The Drawings,* (exh. cat) Whitney Museum of American Art, N.Y., 1979

Dehner, Dorothy, foreword to *John Graham's "Systems and Dialectics of Art,"* Marcia Epstein Allentuck, The Johns Hopkins Press, 1971

— "Memories of Jan Matulka," in *Jan Matulka, 1890-1972,* (exh. cat.) Smithsonian Institution Press, Washington, D.C., 1980

— "Reminiscences," in *Prospect Mountain Sculpture Show, An Homage to David Smith,* (exh. cat.) Lake George Arts Project, Lake George, N.Y., 1979

Fry, Edward T., *David Smith* (exh. cat.) Solomon R. Guggenheim Foundation, N.Y., 1969

Gray, Cleve, ed., *David Smith by David Smith,* Holt, Rinehart and Winston, N.Y., 1968

Greenberg, Clement, review of "American Sculpture of Our Time" exhibition, Willard and Buchhotz Galleries, N.Y., *The Nation,* Vol. 156 No. 4, January 23, 1943, pp. 140-141

— review of "The Sculpture of David Smith" exhibition, Willard and Buchholz Galleries, N.Y., *The Nation,* Vol. 162, No. 4, January 26, 1946, pp. 109-110

— review of "The Whitney Annual," N.Y., *The Nation,* Vol. 164, No. 14, April 5, 1947 p. 405

— review of "David Smith" exhibition, Willard Gallery, N.Y., *The Nation,* Vol. 164, No. 16, April 19, 1947, pp. 459-460

— "Present Prospects of American Painting and Sculpture," Horizon, No. 93-94, October 1947, pp. 20-30

— "The New Sculpture," *Partisan Review,* Vol. 16, No. 6, June 1949, pp. 637-642. (Revised in *Art and Culture,* Beacon Press, Boston, 1961)

— "David Smith," *Art in America,* Vol. 44, No. 4, Winter 1956-57, pp. 30-33, 66. Reprinted *Art in America,* Vol. 51, No. 4, August 1963, pp. 112-117. (Revised in *Art and Culture,* Beacon Press, Boston, 1961.)

— "David Smith's New Sculpture," *Art International,* Vol. 8, No. 4, May 1964, pp. 35-37

Krauss, Rosalind E., *David Smith, Eight Early Works, 1935-38,* (exh. cat.) Marlborough-Gerson Gallery, N.Y., 1967

— *David Smith, Small Sculptures of the Mid-Forties,* (exh. cat.) Marlborough-Gerson Gallery, N.Y., 1968

— *Terminal Iron Works, The Sculpture of David Smith,* The M.I.T. Press, Cambridge, Mass. and London, England, 1971

— *The Sculpture of David Smith, A Catalogue Raisonné,* Garland Publishing, Inc., N.Y., and London, 1977

Lawrence, Ellen; Barkley, Lisa; Clapp, Eleanor; Danto, Sally; Feder, Carrie, *Graham, Gorky, Smith and Davis in the Thirties,* (exh. cat.) Brown University, Providence, R.I., 1977

McClintic, Miranda, *David Smith, The Hirshhorn Museum and Sculpture Garden Collection* (exh. cat.) Smithsonian Institution Press, Washington, D.C., 1979

McCoy, Garnett, ed. *David Smith,* Praeger Publishers, N.Y. and Washington, 1973

David Smith 1906 - 1965, (exh. cat.) Museum of Modern Art, N.Y., 1966

O'Hara, Frank, *Art Chronicles 1954-1966,* George Braziller, N.Y., 1975

Valentiner, Wilhelm R., *The Sculpture of David Smith* (exh. cat.) Willard and Buchholz Gallery, N.Y., 1946